LETTERS OF CHARLES DEMUTH, AMERICAN ARTIST, 1883–1935

EDITED BY BRUCE KELLNER

for The Demuth Foundation, Lancaster, Pennsylvania

WITH ASSESSMENTS OF HIS WORK
BY HIS CONTEMPORARIES:

A. E. Gallatin, Angela E. Hagen, Marsden Hartley, Helen Henderson, Henry McBride, Carl Van Vechten, Rita Wells, Willard Huntington Wright

TEMPLE UNIVERSITY PRESS
PHILADELPHIA

LETTERS OF

CHARLES DEMUTH

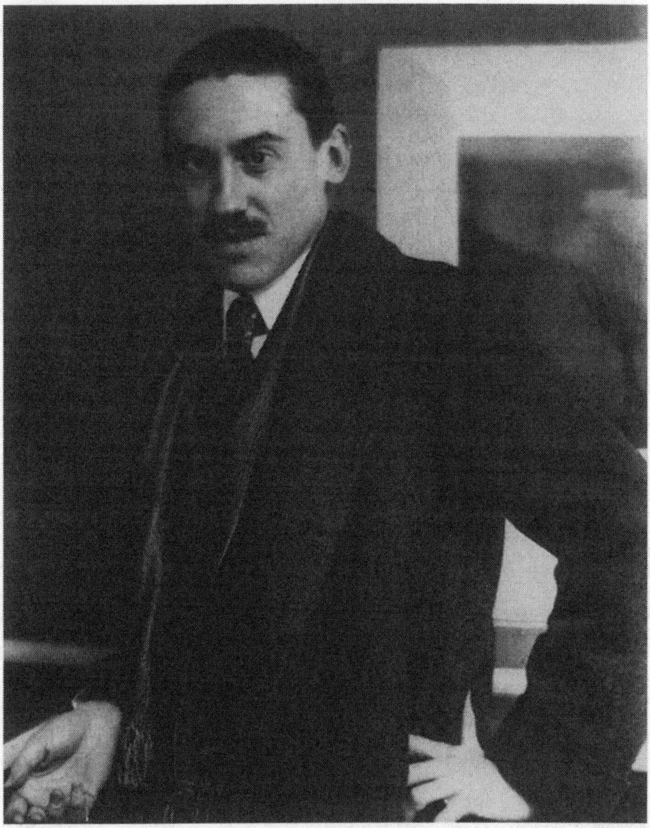

AMERICAN ARTIST, 1883–1935

Temple University Press, Philadelphia 19122

Published 2000
Printed in the United States of America

∞ The paper used in this publication meets the requirements of the American National Standard for Information Sciences—Permanence of Paper for Printed Library Materials, ANSI Z39.48–1984.

Library of Congress Cataloging-in-Publication Data

Demuth, Charles, 1883–1935.
[Correspondence. Selections]
Letters of Charles Demuth, American artist, 1883–1935 : with assessments of his work by his contemporaries . . . / edited by Bruce Kellner for The Demuth Foundation, Lancaster, Pennsylvania.
p. cm.
"A.E. Gallatin, Angela E. Hagen, Marsden Hartley, Helen Henderson, Henry McBride, Carl Van Vechten, Rita Wells, Willard Huntington Wright."
Includes index.
ISBN 1-56639-780-4 (cloth : alk. paper) — ISBN 1-56639-781-2 (paper: alk. paper)
1. Demuth, Charles, 1883–1935—Correspondence. 2. Artists—United States—Correspondence. I. Kellner, Bruce. II. Demuth Foundation. III. Title.

ND237.D36 A3 2000
759.13—dc21
[B] 99-461967

Title page photo: Charles Demuth, circa 1916 (courtesy Yale University Collection of American Literature, Beinecke Rare Book and Manuscript Library)

ISBN 13: 978-1-56639-781-0 (paper: alk. paper)

061610-P

Demuth keeps pretty well, and is working a little. . . . He is a magician. All things considered, there is no better artist in America.

—CHARLES DANIEL TO FERDINAND HOWALD, 1924

My grocery boy contemplates my acrobats, painted by Demuth, and asks:

"Did you paint that?"

"No."

"Thought perhaps you did. I could see it wasn't done by a professional."

—CARL VAN VECHTEN, *NOTEBOOKS*, 1930

CONTENTS

ACKNOWLEDGMENTS

I acknowledge with gratitude the following sources of the letters and other material:

For letters to or from Augusta Demuth, Edward Fisk, A. E. Gallatin, Ferdinand Howald, and Robert Josephy: Archives of American Art, Smithsonian Institution, through Harris Arnold.

For letters to Muriel Draper, Edna Kenton, Henry McBride, Georgia O'Keeffe, Agnes Boulton O'Neill, Eugene O'Neill, Gertrude Stein, Ettie Stettheimer, Alfred Stieglitz, Scofield Thayer, and Carl Van Vechten; for selections from "Farewell, Charles" by Marsden Hartley; and for a photograph of Charles Demuth: Yale University Collection of American Literature, Beinecke Rare Book and Manuscript Library. The photograph was made circa 1916, either by Alfred Stieglitz or by Paul Strand; extant prints do not offer conclusive evidence to identify the photographer more specifically.

For a letter to John Reed: by permission of the Houghton Library, Harvard University.

For letters to George Biddle: the Library of Congress.

For a letter to Carl Van Vechten: New York Public Library,

Astor, Lenox, and Tilden Foundations, Manuscripts and Archives Division, courtesy of the Van Vechten Trust.

For letters to Walter Arensberg, Fiske Kimball, and Henry Ernest Schnakenberg: Arensberg Archives © Philadelphia Museum of Art.

For letters to Juliana Force: Archives of the Whitney Museum of American Art.

For letters to William Carlos Williams: printed with the permission of The Poetry/Rare Books Collection, University Libraries, State University of New York at Buffalo.

For letters to Augusta Demuth: the late Pauline Stauffer.

For letters about Demuth from Henry McBride, essays by McBride, and other essays in *Creative Art:* courtesy of Maximilian H. Miltzlaff.

The letters and other writings of Charles Demuth are published with the permission of the Demuth Foundation, Lancaster, Pennsylvania.

I regret that thirty-six letters from Demuth to Alfred C. Barnes, 1919–1923, were unavailable for inclusion because the Barnes Foundation demanded alterations in my annotations that I could not accept. Demuth's story is incomplete without these letters; Barnes was a loyal friend and mentor from circa 1905 when they met until Demuth's death in 1935.

Charles Demuth: Behind the Laughing Mask by Emily Farnham (Norman: University of Oklahoma Press, 1971), *Charles Demuth* by Barbara Haskell (New York: Whitney Museum of American Art/Harry N. Abrams, 1987), the unpublished daybooks of Carl Van Vechten (1922–1930), *Strange Bedfellows: The First American Avant-Garde* by Steven Watson (New York: Abbeville, 1991), *Speaking for Vice: Homosexuality in the Art of Charles Demuth, Marsden Hartley, and the First American Avant-Garde* by Jonathan Weinberg (New Haven: Yale University Press, 1993), and *Charles Demuth: Poster Portraits, 1923–1929* by Robin Jaffee Frank (New

Haven: Yale University Press, 1994) were of inestimable value in annotating these letters.

I am grateful to Corinne Woodcock, executive director of the Demuth Foundation, for her cooperation and practical assistance; to Cheri Markowitz, former director of the Foundation, for her wise counsel and enthusiasm for this project from its inception; to Carol Morgan, retired director of the Foundation, for her diligence in solving thick mysteries on the thinnest of leads, and for a scrupulous copyediting for factual accuracy; to the staff in Ganser Library at Millersville University for many favors; to the Lancaster County Historical Society, the Lancaster County Public Library, the Cape Ann Historical Society, and the National Portrait Gallery for research; to my friend J. Joel Farber for his genial patience with my slow progress in word processing and in helping me solve various technical mysteries.

For information, encouragement, and favors major or minor or both, many thanks to the late Donald Angus, Ellen Arnold Aspinall, Currell Beneck, Lisa Browar, Edward Burns, Steven Centola, Ellen Cordes, Ulla Dydo, Sylvia Evans, Betsy Fahlman, Jeffrey M. Flannery, Sybil Freeman, Debra Greenleaf-Campbell, Jean Gromoll, Harry G. Heise, Jeanne Herman, Pat Hines, Sally Jarvis, Steve Jones, Hans Kellner, Gerald Lestz, Barbara Lewis, Charles Maser, Mimi McQueen, Theresa Melchiorre, Timothy Miller, Maximilian H. Miltzlaff, Bart Murphy, Francis Naumann, Richard Newman, Priscilla Oppenheimer, Jeff Peabody, Carole Pesner, Wendy Wick Reaves, Ginger Shelley, the late Joseph Solomon, Steven Watson, Jonathan Weinberg, Patricia Willis, Donald Windham, Tim Young, Dale Ziegler, and Marie Zubatsky.

Finally, I thank my friend and fellow former board member at the Demuth Foundation, Margaret C. Woodbridge. She meticulously checked copies of the original letters, notes, and cards in Demuth's handwriting as I read aloud from the transcripts, to correct errors and verify accuracy, to test Demuth's punctuation against our joint common sense, and to judge the necessity of footnotes for amplification. I am in her permanent debt.

Bruce Kellner
Lancaster, Pennsylvania

INTRODUCTION

The American painter Charles Demuth—admired and respected for his Precisionist cityscapes and poster portraits; his exquisite watercolors of flowers, fruits, and vegetables; his freewheeling drawings and paintings of acrobats, vaudeville performers, sailors, saloons, bathhouses, and beaches; and his illustrations for books—aspired to be a writer as well as an artist.

The few surviving examples of his literary efforts suggest that he was wise to stick to painting, although his letters to his friends offer a tantalizing portrait of a remarkable figure. Only a few brief pieces found their way into print, as brochure notes for exhibitions or similar appreciations, including an attempt to explain his own work; but Demuth's play about art and its criticism, *The Azure Adder,* was published in the January 1913 issue of *The Glebe,* the Imagist "little magazine" turned out by printer-designer May Ray and poet Alfred Kreymborg.

Simultaneous with that publication, Demuth encountered Post-Impressionist and Cubist painting during his second trip to Paris, in the salon of Gertrude Stein at 27 rue de Fleurus, notably the work of Paul Cezanne, Henri Matisse, Pablo Picasso, and

Juan Gris. A month later the now legendary Sixty-ninth Regimental Armory Exhibition stunned the New York art community, introducing this country to the same new waves in modern art that had already engulfed Demuth.

Although the direct influence of these movements on his own painting would not be immediately felt, their effect was sufficient to motivate him to begin several years of commuting between Lancaster, Pennsylvania, where he was born on 8 November 1883, and various locales where the cultural, intellectual, and sexual climates were more congenial.

Beginning in 1914, he frequently spent his summers in Provincetown on Cape Cod, where he knew many painters and writers of the period and was involved in the founding of the Provincetown Players. Those intermittent holidays ended only a year before his death in 1935.

He was close enough to Philadelphia for day trips to see members of the art colony he had known since his days as a student there at the Pennsylvania Academy of the Fine Arts. Also, he was a welcome visitor to Merion, Pennsylvania, on the outskirts of Philadelphia, at the home of Dr. Alfred C. Barnes, whose private collection of modern art rivaled that of any museum in the country at the time and included dozens of Demuth's own watercolors. Friend as well patron, Barnes was largely responsible for persuading the artist to undergo medical treatment for diabetes.

Demuth went periodically (and sometimes weekly) to New York, where Alfred Stieglitz eventually included him in his stable of painters, along with Arthur Dove, Marsden Hartley, John Marin, and Georgia O'Keeffe. During those years, Demuth was a regular guest at three historic salons: that of Mabel Dodge (later Luhan), who held court for poets and anarchists alike from 1913; that of Walter and Louise Arensberg, who collected contemporary art, endorsed avant-garde music, and supported French Dadaist Marcel Duchamp; and that of the Stettheimer sisters—Florine painted, Ettie wrote, Carrie presided—who cultivated a rarefied high bohemian garden above the gaiety of the Teens and the roar of the Twenties. He was an intimate member of all three, but he did not spend all of his time in such cosmopolitan atmospheres.

Usually he stayed at the Brevoort Hotel, a popular lodging in Greenwich Village for artists and writers at the time. In the fall of 1915, however, Demuth took a studio apartment for the season, on Washington Square, near several of his regular hangouts. The Golden Swan—its popular backroom was always referred to as the Hell Hole—stood on the corner of Fourth Street and Sixth Avenue; later, Eugene O'Neill thinly disguised it as the setting for his 1946 play, *The Iceman Cometh.* Louis Holladay (or Holliday) ran a café on Washington Square South, called "The Sixty." His sister Polly Holladay had several restaurants, but the first and best known was in the basement of the Liberal Club on MacDougal Street, next door to the Provincetown Players' theater, where Christine and Louis Ell's restaurant later occupied the second floor. The Purple Pup and Romany Marie's were other familiar saloons. Also, Demuth's apartment was an easy subway ride to his favorite black hangouts, at Marshall's Hotel on West Fifty-third Street, in the area popularly known as Black Bohemia, and Baron Wilkins's Little Savoy on West Thirty-fifth Street. And there were several homosexual haunts along the way, including the Lafayette Baths south of Cooper Square, an easy stroll from the Brevoort. He memorialized many of these sites in his work, though apparently for the amusement of his friends and himself rather than for the public.

As for foreign travel, Demuth returned to Europe for a third trip in the fall of 1921—he had been in Paris in 1907–1908 for five months, and again for about a year and a half in 1912–1914, with side trips to London and Berlin—and with his friend and fellow painter Marsden Hartley he took a painting holiday to Bermuda in February 1917.

In between these jaunts, he returned to Lancaster to recuperate from the diabetes that began to weaken him before he was forty. (Demuth was one of the first diabetics to take insulin injections, initially every two hours.) He had an unusually strong relationship with his mother—in letters to others she referred to him as "the boy" when he was nearly forty years old—and continued to live with her in the townhouse where he had been reared, the only child of Augusta and tobacconist Ferdinand Demuth. Both his studio and his bedroom—which opened off his mother's bedroom—looked out on her extensive garden behind the house, which served as subject matter for many of his paintings. Demuth was apparently content with this arrangement, but he referred to his hometown as "the province," and he titled one of his paintings of its grain elevators *My Egypt,* implying that he was in self-imposed bondage. For the last fifteen years of his life, he was obliged to stay in Lancaster most of the time, except when the pull of New York or Provincetown grew too strong, or during periods of recuperation in the Physiatric Institute in Morristown, New Jersey, the sanatorium where he had first been treated with monitored dieting in 1922 and then received insulin the following year. Financially as well as emotionally, he was supported during these ordeals by his friend and mentor, the eccentric art collector Dr. Alfred C. Barnes.

Charles Demuth had begun painting when he was a child and by the age of thirty had started selling his work through Charles Daniel, a New York saloonkeeper turned art dealer, indeed the only art dealer other than Alfred Stieglitz who concentrated on contemporary American painting. Within another decade collectors had begun to buy Demuth's work, some of his paintings had entered the permanent collections of museums, and he moved as easily in arts and letters circles as he did in speakeasies in Greenwich Village and Harlem. In New York, he counted many celebrated artists and writers among his friends; in Lancaster, he was an intimate of those who must have been considered, by his fellow townspeople, as that sleepy city's "fast set."

Charles Demuth died shortly before his fifty-second birthday, exhausted by the disease that had wasted his body but not his talent. Death came in his second-floor bedroom. Its windows had offered him a view, in the near distance, of the steeple of Trinity Lutheran Church. At closer range, he had seen the abundant flowers in his mother's gardens fill their brick-lined beds from season to season throughout his life. He drew on such scenes for both the Precisionist modernism of his oils and for the romantic extravagance of his watercolors. He left behind a remarkable body of work that is now disseminated among most major museums, and some minor ones, across the country, and he has been the subject of several scholarly studies.

An aspiring writer with several addresses may correspond with friends; an aspiring writer confined for protracted periods of time in a small town or a sanatorium because of his chronic poor health is even more likely to do so. Unlike Demuth's other efforts with words, he was always able to convey an ebullience and ease of expression in his correspondence, whether he was writing to his mother, his mentors, or intimate friends. In business correspondence, too, his wry sense of humor was apparent, although even with his closest correspondents he could be self-effacing, elliptical, and guarded about his private life.

Indeed, descriptions of Charles Demuth by his contemporaries might serve as illustrations for these letters. He was not effeminate, as has been sometimes suggested, but merely odd in his manner and movements and eccentric in his dress—an off-horse in a one-horse town and a fashionably high-stepping strutter out of town. During the Teens and Twenties he often wore a brightly colored tie about his waist in place of a belt, following a fashion trend among effete young men in New York. He sported a Homburg. He wore spats. Demuth was a homosexual dandy, with a whinnying laugh and a high-pitched voice, black hair like patent leather that he slicked back after spitting on his hands, a reddish moustache, and a sweetly malicious wit.

On Cape Cod, in New York, in Paris, even in Lancaster, he was much engaged—part of the time, at least—in homosexual circles. It is difficult for some members of subsequent generations to grasp the closed system through which unspoken sexual identity was communicated during the early years of this century. George Chauncey, Jr.'s *Gay New York* (New York: Basic Books, 1994), a luminously informative study of the subject, explains for all readers but prurient ones why there is so little evidence to account for many relationships that may have existed between homosexuals at the time. It is possible for men—heterosexual as well as homosexual—to form intimate, nonsexual friendships as well as sexual ones with other men. Those few instances when Demuth's letters engage in camp references and observations to suggest his homosexuality are sufficiently inconsequential to merit no especial attention. He was decorous, he was discreet.

Demuth suffered from a limp as the result of the then unrecognized Perthes' disease, in which the growth of the hip ball is arrested in male children. He controlled his uncertain gait by using a cane, although he employed it as often as a prop for his asymmetrical stance as he did as a support for his undulating gait. He used his expressive hands, with their attenuated fingers, when he spoke, and usually he clutched a white handkerchief that he held to his mouth during bursts of merriment. Contemporaries later observed that in public, at least, he seemed almost always to be laughing. His piercing, black eyes were not crossed, as some people have contended, but they did carry a decided cast—inherited from his father—that gave him a slightly maniacal look. Often Charles Demuth appeared to be staring in two different directions at the same time. Maybe he was.

The emotional and physical divisions in his life—between his devotion to his mother in the quiet and conventional atmosphere of his "province" and to the freewheeling social milieu in the low saloons and high salons of New York—was as clear in his askant stare as it still is in his letters and in the rich legacy of his art.

The bulk of Charles Demuth's correspondence seems not to have survived, though extensive exchanges of letters with Barnes, A. E. Gallatin, Stieglitz, and Scofield Thayer suggest that he was a prolific writer, channeling his early urges toward literature into letters to friends and associates. It is likely, for example, that he would have written regularly to his mother during his periods away from his home in Lancaster, although only four of his letters and some brief cards to her have survived. Just a few letters to his early friend, William Carlos Williams, survive, and none to later, more intimate friends like Marcel Duchamp, Marsden Hartley, and Robert Locher.

Demuth was a casual correspondent, slapdash in matters of form and diction, but he was enthusiastic in expressing himself about his art and the art of his contemporaries, as well as about whatever facets of his life he wished to share with his correspondents. Many times his thoughts run away with his words, and the result is an exuberant run-on sentence or a series of impressionistic fragments, dashed off in a nearly inarticulate eagerness to share his ideas. Indeed, his disregard for conventional sentences allows his written words to reflect what might have been his spoken voice: halting, rushing, interrupting itself with verbal circumlocutions. This sometimes leads to confusion; occasionally, his erratic punctuation makes it impossible to trace the antecedents of his pronouns or the subjects to which his verbs belong.

In view of Demuth's slender talents at verbal endeavors, it is always surprising to recall that during his early years he aspired to be a poet and playwright, and that for a time he was torn between devoting himself to painting or to writing. His imaginative efforts are labored, and his attempts at art criticism are affectionate but undisciplined. Although the breathless conversational tone that informs his letters is as charming as it is appropriate in correspondence, his brief forays into public declarations are influenced by a fin-de-siècle sensibility long out of fashion, at least in professional prose. His artistic credo, published in the September 1929 issue of *Creative Art,* for example, gives some indication of his limitations as a writer, and he had some trouble in writing it at all, as his letter to Alfred Stieglitz circa 12 December 1928 indicates. "To me words explain too much and say too little," he observes in his essay, not an inappropriate observation about his own words:

ACROSS A GRECO IS WRITTEN

I have been urged by Mr. Lee Simonson,— who if he would, could do it much better—I too have other pleasures—to write about my own paintings.

At the start: "Why?"

Haven't I, in a way, painted them?

Poems have been written by painters about their paintings, I know, and—I have heard painters, in my own time, speak excitedly about their own work. Colour and line can say quite a bit, unaided by words, when used by one for whom they are a means of expression. Words are not to me a means. I can only paint. Many days I don't feel that this is true—this: "I can write." To me words explain too much and say too little.

If I could write and believed in having a cause, even a good cause—well, certainly I would write about the paintings which are being done, at the moment, in my country. Good things many of them, and, some to me, great works. But I must leave "this cause" to time; time the final critic and only creator of legend. I feel certain time and I shall agree.

The idea of having painters write about their own paintings is to me not one which is likely to produce great results—add to the medium of words. And unless this addition is accomplished, why write? There comes to my mind only one thing written by a painter about his drawings which really added to literature—it is called "Venus and Tannhauser" [by Aubrey Beardsley]. However!

Across the final surface—the touchable bloom, if it were a peach—of any fine painting is written for those who dare to read that which the painter knew, that which he hoped to find out, or, that which he—whatever!

Across a Greco, across a Blake, across a Rubens, across a Watteau, across a Beardsley is written in larger letters than any printed page will ever dare to hold, or, Broadway facade or roof support what its creator had to say about it. To translate these painted sentences, whatever they may be, into words—well, try it. With the best of luck the "sea change" will be great. Or, granting a translation of this kind were successful what would you have but what was there already, and as readable—and perhaps, on repetition, a trifle boring.

Paintings are; and, I call complete drawings, paintings, too, to be looked at. If the "inner eye" does not glitter before certain contemporary "Calla Lilies," certain American water-colours, certain of Florine [Stettheimer]'s, or Peggy [Bacon]'s portraits, added physical words will not cause it to glitter—even though spoken or written by Pater or Joyce. Your choice—ladies!

For the painter, paintings are, wet or dry, just paintings. They are not arguments. They are signs on the way to that supposed Nirvana; Culture. They are not—however, this must be printed in our new world, so perhaps that: "They are not," cannot be said.

Paintings must be looked at and looked at and looked at—they, I think, the good ones, like it. They must be

> understood, and that's not the word, either, through the eyes. No writing, no talking, no singing, no dancing will explain them. They are the final, the 'nth whoopee of sight. A water-melon, a kiss may be fair, but after all have other uses. "Look at that!" is all that can be said before a great painting, at least, by those who really see it.
>
> "And cannot words, written or spoken, help those who have partial or little sight for painting?"
>
> My answer to this question is: No. Only prayer, and looking, and looking at painting and—prayer can help.
>
> But those two will help—You who do not see pictures. They will help—and some day, when before a painting, you will see it without thought of the name of its author, or amount paid. You will see it in its glory—in the world of paint. You will have received the stigmata.

Fortunately, Demuth's crabbed inversions and tortured syntax, together with the physical and mental exertion he suffered in writing, persuaded him to abandon his literary aspirations. More than once he speaks of how difficult writing is for him, although his letters suggest, too, that he genuinely enjoyed the now largely outmoded means of communication.

This book includes all of Charles Demuth's letters that are currently available for publication. Though brief, it illuminates his paintings as well as his character. In both, he was an American original.

A NOTE ON EDITING

The letters in this selection are transcribed essentially as Demuth wrote them, although when necessary for sense—and to avoid riddling the pages with [*sic*]—I have silently corrected an amazing range of errors in his frequently phonetic spelling. I have preserved his English spellings, which were popular among the intelligentsia during the Twenties, and his erratic interchange of *all right* and *alright,* sometimes in the same letter. Demuth's catalog of spellings for Georgia O'Keeffe's last name is too varied and even hilarious to be entirely accidental, and so I have reproduced these inspirations as well. She is almost always referred to with his private nickname for her, G'Keeffe, but with a number of variations. I have corrected his occasional grammatical slips in number, agreement, and tenses, and I have opted for his use or nonuse of hyphens in certain words, like *watercolour* and *water-colour,* depending on which version predominated throughout the letters.

Charles Demuth's punctuation might be charitably described as inventive. When it confuses his content, or seems likely to impair the reader's progress, I have silently altered it, preserving his idiosyncrasies when it was feasible to do so. His routine use of what can only be called a new mark of punctuation—the "commadash"—obfuscates more often than it clarifies his meaning, and I have frequently dropped it, as well as many of his constant, unnecessary commas. On the other hand, one of his latter-day admirers has suggested that Demuth's commadash might be a method of handwriting developed as a consequence of his being an artist—a kind of compulsion to sketch the ideas he was striving to articulate. Not a bad defense.

He seems to have used both commas and commadashes to stand in for semicolons, colons, and periods, as well as for deep breaths; also, he seems to have used them to mark time or change subjects rather than to emphasize his content. Once or twice, however, I have even been obliged to employ his commadash, where he himself did not use it, to try to clarify the fits and starts of a passage. In turn, his meaning is sometimes complicated because of his arch diction and convoluted qualifying phrases and clauses, together with his frequent dropping of conventional first-person pronouns. A sufficient number of his idiosyncracies remain, however, to suggest something about the way he may have expressed himself in conversation. If he spoke the way he wrote, there must have always been a circuitous path winding its way through his speech, with a breathless quality to its delivery.

I have preserved Demuth's abbreviations unless they might be confusing, in which case I have enclosed completed words in brackets; I have added obviously missing words, also in brackets; and, admitting defeat only after three other people familiar with Demuth's handwriting gave up too, I have bracketed some words with a question mark or, indeed, bracketed the word *word* when nothing suggested itself.

I have identified most people and unfamiliar places initially in footnotes, subsequently bracketing missing names until the person referred to has been clearly established through repetition; others, usually in offhand historical references, I have spelled out in full in Demuth's text on their first occurrence, in brackets. The reader may assume that unidentified or incomplete names have proven untraceable, and that unexplained cryptic references must retain their mystery, since little of Demuth's incoming correspondence—which might have answered such questions—seems to have been preserved.

I have supplied identifications for the layman, not for the scholar, and therefore the full names of many of them—for example, English poet William Blake, American painter Benjamin West, or American poet Wallace Stevens—will be obvious and even redundant to many readers.

I have followed Demuth's lead in putting all titles in quotation marks when he neglected in some cases to supply them. Except for telegrams, nearly all of Demuth's letters have been transcribed from his holograph, either from original copies or from xeroxes, but the dates and places of origin are often incomplete, and postmarks are sometimes indecipherable; the addresses are sometimes imprinted on his stationery and sometimes written out, complete or abbreviated. Unless otherwise noted, all letters are return addressed to Demuth's residence, 118 East King Street, Lancaster, Pennsylvania. Demuth's penmanship was usually clear but erratic; it could differ radically from one sequential letter to another, so that undated letters cannot always be dated on the basis of physical similarity to others by chronology. For the sake of conformity, I have standardized dates without indicating variations, and without the use of brackets to indicate my additions, unless of course the place and date were conjectural. I have adopted uniform punctuation for salutations and closings in accordance with those that Demuth most frequently employed.

In no case have I bowdlerized the letters in any way. Demuth was a decorous correspondent and expressed any scabrous observations through innuendo and indirection, although his unbuttoned humor could on occasion bubble over to mask what must have been a difficult life.

LETTERS OF CHARLES DEMUTH,
AMERICAN ARTIST, 1883–1935

TO MRS. C. L. EHLEN[1]

14 February 1896

If of me you sometimes think
Send me back my bow of pink.
If to me your heart is true
Send me back my bow of blue.
If you are another girls fellow
Send me back my bow of yellow.
If to me your heart is dead
Send me back my bow of red.

[unsigned]

TO WILLIAM CARLOS WILLIAMS[2]

17 September 1907

Carlos, Carlos, how good your letter did sound. I want to answer it before I sail & know if I let it go much longer it will be impossible.

In about two weeks I'll be starting from home for Philadelphia: from there I sail on the 4th of October.

[1]A neighbor who lived at 202 East King Street. On this postcard, Augusta Demuth wrote: "Charlie made a number of these valentines at 11 years." According to Emily Farnham's *Charles Demuth: Behind the Laughing Mask* (Norman: University of Oklahoma Press, 1971), Demuth wrote postcards to his family from Atlantic City in July and August 1895; she cites Richard Weyand's scrapbooks as her source. Some of the Weyand material disappeared after his death in 1956; the remainder is now in the Beinecke Library at Yale University This valentine is the earliest of Charles Demuth's "letters."

[2]American poet and pediatrician. He and Demuth met in Philadelphia when they were residents in the same boarding house; their friendship endured until Demuth's death.

But getting back to your affairs, you [have] no idea how your letter affected me. I have always felt that it would happen to you some day—that you would simply have to write. However hearing that it would happen this minute was grand news. There's a young chap in New York now, his name is George Frederick—he has written some very good things, poems. He had them published in the spring—the collection is called "Nineva." I wish you would read some of them if you can get ahold of the book. I have never met him but have several very good friends whom are also friends of his. You may not like his stuff, I can't tell, not having talked art to you for so long a time.

I will not be able to see you before I go—yes, it is too bad. Still Carlos when I come back—when I come back—well, we may both have a start in a small way then. I will be over a year at least, perhaps longer. You see, I have just a certain amount of money to spend while abroad & when that is gone I must come back. If I can make it last over the year, of course I'll stay. So I may see [*Edd?*]—who can tell?

And Carlos even though nothing happens after your six months work in Boston don't give up, will you? It's worth all the money & tears, after all. To feel the joys of creating for a single moment seems to repay one for a year's work. Of course, I know, so do you, that at times it's hell. When you feel like giving it all up & then you think, but what would become of me if I really was made to give it up for ever. Heaven be praised neither one of us will meet such a fate—I hope.

Ever since I started to write this letter parts of what will follow keep popping into my head:

"High, Higher than seventh heaven above,
Low, Lower than deepest hell beneath,
We rise and fall—you & I.
In ecstasy more full,

In sorrow more intense,
Than all these fools could ever guess,
We rise and fall—you & I.
Back and forth—
Forth to the Idea,
Back—to where?
No place or mark is there!
All this for beauty
Veiled, eternal, sure,
The essence of the morning's mist,
Of feeding flocks & lovers' close embrace."

I can't remember whose this is—perhaps they're mine[1]—one does fight at times especially when you expect to see the sights of Paris within the month.

Good-bye, good-bye with the very best wishes.

Demuth

TO ALFRED STIEGLITZ[2]

19 April 1916

My dear Stieglitz:—

The photographs came to-day. They are fine, aren't they?

Hartley[3] will tell you how anxious, after seeing his, one time abroad, I always was for you sometime to do me. And now it's done!

[1]The poet has not been identified; Demuth may have written the lines himself.

[2]American photographer and art gallery impresario, and Demuth's strongest professional mentor. They met first through Stieglitz's 291 Gallery in New York; later, Stieglitz regularly featured Demuth's paintings in exhibitions at his Intimate Gallery and American Place. The bulk of Demuth's extant letters were written to Stieglitz.

[3]American artist Marsden Hartley, whom Demuth had met in Paris, and through whom he met Gertrude Stein in the winter of 1912–1913. There is no evidence that they were ever lovers, but their homosexuality doubtless influenced their long-standing, intimate friendship. For a study of its influence on their work, see Jonathan Weinberg, *Speaking for Vice: Homosexuality in the Art of Charles Demuth, Marsden Hartley, and the First American Avant-Garde* (New Haven: Yale University Press, 1993).

Thank you very much for them and may I too thank you, here, for the something which I found so often this winter at 291 and which you make so possible.

Best regards for Mrs. Stieglitz.[1]

As ever,
Demuth

TO JOHN REED[2]

[circa autumn 1916]

Jack:—

The [Provincetown Players] meeting I am told is to be at your rooms to-night.

You might tell said meeting that I will be in my province until November 10th or 15th. After all there is no place like one's own home for a slow season; the only possible place for a complete "get away" from the "drama" (in America) and artists of all kind! You need not mention this last outburst to the gathered elders.

How are you? I hope o.k. Best for Louise.[3]

As ever,
Demuth

[1]Emmeline Obermeyer, who divorced Stieglitz in 1924; he then married American painter Georgia O'Keeffe.

[2]American poet, journalist, and anarchist. Reed and Demuth met at the time of the founding of the Provincetown Players on Cape Cod in 1915; the previous summer Demuth had become involved with other artists and writers there. Both Demuth and Reed appeared in plays on Cape Cod in 1915 and 1916; the company took up residence on MacDougal Street in Greenwich Village in the fall of 1916.

[3]American journalist Louise Bryant. She was alternately the lover of Reed, after the breakup of his affair with art patroness Mabel Dodge (later Luhan), and Eugene O'Neill between his first two marriages. Bryant subsequently married Reed; after his death, she married socially prominent American diplomat William Bullitt.

Am inclosing check for four—I think that was the amount, and probably the theater is in need of all it can get.[1]

Demo

TO ALFRED STIEGLITZ
31 December 1916

My dear Stieglitz:—
Wishing you an interesting & happy New Year.

Demuth

I see by the "Sun"[2] that the water-colors are on exhibition. They are really fine to me.

TO HENRY MCBRIDE[3]
[circa early April 1917]

Brevoort House, Fifth Avenue at 8th Street
New York City

My dear McBride:—
A piece of sculpture, called "A Fountain," was entered, by one of our friends, for the Independent Exhibition now open at the Grand Central Palace.[4]

[1]The first New York bill of the Provincetown Players included Eugene O'Neill's *Bound East for Cardiff,* Louise Bryant's *The Game,* and Floyd Dell's *King Arthur's Socks,* not a program likely to draw large audiences. Bryant and Reed soon resigned over policy issues.
[2]The *New York Sun.*
[3]American art critic who wrote regularly for the *New York Sun* and, beginning in 1920, also contributed the monthly column "Modern Art" to the *Dial,* arguably the most significant art and literary journal of the 1920s. McBride was an early supporter of the avant-garde and Demuth's longest-standing professional promoter in print. McBride wrote with only guarded admiration about Demuth's first exhibition, in the fall of 1914; two years later, however, he had become a strong ally.
[4]The French-American artist Marcel Duchamp purchased an ordinary urinal to enter in the exhibition as the sculpture of "Richard Mutt." Stieglitz photographed it extensively, and Demuth wrote a poem about it, published in Duchamp's magazine *Blind Man,* all of which created a minor scandal.

It was not exhibited.

"The Independents," we are now told, have a committee,—or jury, who can decide, "for the good of the exhibition."

We think that a show called "The Super Independents"—or Salon des Refusés—is the next move.

If you think you could do anything with this material for your Sunday article we would appreciate it very much.[1]

Yours sincerely,
C. Demuth

P.S. If you wish any more information please 'phone Marcel Duchamp, 4225 Columbus, or Richard Mutt, 9255 Schuyler.[2]

C.D.[3]

TO HENRY MCBRIDE

[circa 25 November 1917]

Brevoort House, Fifth Avenue at 8th Street
New York City

My dear McBride:—

I wish to thank you for Sunday's.[4]

[1]On 15 April 1917, McBride wrote in his *Sun* column: "The proportion of inoffensive to offensive works is about ten to one, and offensive is meant in the complimentary sense of being challenging."

[2]The second telephone number was that of American writer Louise Norton, who with her husband Allen published the little magazine *Rogue;* later she married avant-garde composer Edgard Varèse.

[3]On 15 July 1917, McBride wrote an extended article in the *Sun* about the negative criticism, in the magazine *Soil,* of the Independent Society as well as of several contemporary artists. He quoted the *Soil* article on Demuth: "There is a little bit of linear product in Demuth's attempts to be peculiar."

[4]On 25 November 1917, McBride wrote an extended article in the *Sun* about Demuth's work, "An Underground Search for Higher Moralities," praising his current popularity with collectors and noting his alliance with Gertrude Stein that linked their attitudes about popular success.

In New York so few get it.

Thank you.

Yours sincerely,
Charles Demuth

TO HENRY MCBRIDE
27 November 1917

Brevoort House, Fifth Avenue at 8th Street
New York City

My dear McBride:—

Miss Stein will laugh if it ever does reach Nimes.[1]

I wish that you would look my drawings over again, and, if you find one, I would like you to take it for your walls, or, for the space you prefer for your pictures.

With my kindest wishes, I remain

Yours sincerely,
C. Demuth

TO HENRY MCBRIDE
9 March 1919

Dear Mr. McBride:—

It was nice to see it traced back to Miss Stein, in the T. N. T. thing in to-day's Sun.[2] In the rush of followers it seems to be quite

[1]During World War I, the experimental expatriate American writer Gertrude Stein, and her companion, Alice B. Toklas, drove a small Ford truck to hospitals all over France, including Nimes, to deliver supplies, through the American Fund for the French Wounded. McBride's *Sun* article on 25 November 1917 refers to this.

[2]*T.N.T.* was a little magazine edited by Man Ray, of which there was a single issue, in 1919. It contained "Vacuum Tires," a poem by Walter Arensberg, which, according to McBride's *Sun* column, was heavily dependent on Gertrude Stein's writing.

the thing to forget or discredit the "great" (please, think of the little dots [i.e., quotation marks] as being used after the manner of Henry James—more or less, entre nous), Gertrude. The idea about Miss Stein and Miss Garden[1] which you had, around Xmas, was amazing!

With best regards—

Sincerely,
Demuth

P.S. Ask Daniel[2] to show you the Bouché canvasses.[3]

TO AGNES BOULTON AND EUGENE O'NEILL[4]

[circa 1919]

Dear Agie & Eugene:—

You see, dearies, I'm back in the province in the garden of my own chateau,— where I'll be for the remaining days of the season. The quiet and yellow velvet old age which I always predicted for myself has started: oh, yes my health is much more advanced than any of my contemporaries! I hope, dear Agie, you are still thin. You are about the only one I could at the moment appear with,— and if we do ever appear the "'90's" will have nothing

[1]Volatile Scots-American opera diva Mary Garden.

[2]Charles Daniel, Demuth's first professional dealer.

[3]French-American painter Louis Bouché.

[4]American playwright whom Demuth had met in Provincetown in 1915. Despite the long-standing story to the contrary, there is no evidence that he and O'Neill had shared a room there over the summer. The following summer Demuth met pulp fiction writer Agnes Boulton, whom O'Neill married in 1919 when she became pregnant.

on us for "delicate mad hands" or having "only having pursued our passing vanities."

Love,
Demuth

Send the other one to Eddy,[1] will you, old dear. C. D.

TO AGNES BOULTON, SHANE,[2] AND EUGENE O'NEILL
[circa late December 1919]

My dear Shane, Agie, Gene:—

I'll put the baby first, I'm sure it is now that way in the house. Too, the times show that it is nicer (although that is hardly the word, nicer), to let the youngest generation "in" than it is to get nervous about them knocking at the door; so, happy new year to Shane first.

My Christmas was quiet in the province as no doubt yours was in Provincetown. That house you have must be fine for winter. Have been thinking of the end of the Cape of late; thinking it would be, perhaps, a help to see it at this season.

It appears that the easiest thing to do, and, I'm afraid this is the thing I do, is to stay on here for a month or six weeks and finish up my present work. I'll try to have February in New York, for what reason I'm sure I don't know, these days of wood-alcohol! I hope we who love drink, for itself, will some time be together in a fair country full of the "Triu-bang."

What of the plays?

[1]American painter Edward Fisk, for whom Demuth enclosed a photograph. Fisk later married Boulton's sister and became a teacher at the University of Kentucky. He is one of nineteen people of whom Demuth painted "portraits," although that includes his "poster portraits," which were, in effect, portraits of the work or personalities of various artists and writers. Fisk and Demuth had first met in Paris in 1907.
[2]O'Neill's second child; his first, Eugene Jr., was the son of Kathleen Jenkins O'Neill.

Have seen Marsden,— [1] but he was there that day, so this is no news.

Will see you in town in February, I hope. Perhaps I'll go to England. I must have a drink on some street corner of the world soon,— or bust.

Many happy New Years for Poppa & Mamma & to Susan and Gig[2] if you see them.

Yours,
Demuth

TO WALTER ARENSBERG[3]
[undated, prior to 1921]

My dear Walter:—

When in town last week called you several times & one evening, Spencer[4] & I came to see you. Then I was told you were in Boston.

I had a photo of a small cupboard, one which hangs on the wall, early American, which I wanted to show to you. There is a woman here who has several very good early American pieces. Can't you motor up & see them? That is better really than seeing

[1]Marsden Hartley and Demuth had become warm friends; they roomed together briefly in John Reed's house in Provincetown in the fall of 1916; then Hartley went to Bermuda to paint, where Demuth joined him in February 1917.

[2]American writer Susan Glaspell and her husband, American writer George Cram Cook, who had founded the Provincetown Players.

[3]The Arensberg Circle of artists and writers was headed by an eccentric, avant-garde poet and patron, heir to his family's fortune from a Pittsburgh crucible company. Walter supported galleries and little magazines like *Rogue* and *Blind Man* (to which Demuth contributed), financed painter's careers, and, with his wife Louise, collected art. At the time, he was much interested in American folk art and furniture. The Arensbergs moved permanently from New York to Los Angeles in 1921. Demuth's handwriting suggests that he wrote this letter circa 1917.

[4]American Precisionist painter Niles Spencer.

photographs. As by train is only 3½ hours. That is if you want any more pieces. There is a very good small blue table, pine.

I will be in town again after Easter, and will bring the photograph which I had, that is if you don't come up before. I think you really must own this table & cupboard.

Yours sincerely,
Demuth

TO ALFRED STIEGLITZ
2 January 1921

Dear Stieglitz:—

I did want you really to have that one, and was sorry not to see you, but most of the time, well,— I'm not up to doing very much about anything.[1]

Will see you I hope some time soon when things are more or less,— more or less,— god knows what.

Thanks for the nice note.

Wishing you a very Happy New Year, and O'Keif[2] the same.

As always,
Demuth

[1]During the summer of 1920, Demuth first experienced indications of serious illness and left Cape Cod for a hasty return to Lancaster. Just over a month after writing this letter, Demuth first consulted Richard Reisman, M.D., at the Physiatric Clinic in Morristown, New Jersey, regarding what proved to be diabetes.

[2]American painter Georgia O'Keeffe, whose name nearly everybody misspelled in the early years of her career. Demuth seems to have done this on purpose after a while, eventually preferring his own invention, "G'Keeffe," to other variations. She admired Demuth, both as a person and as an artist; he willed all of his unsold oil paintings to her, and she dispersed them among museums and libraries.

TO SCOFIELD THAYER[1]

postmark 28 February 1921

My dear Thayer:—

When in London look up Lovat Frazer[2] & Charles Winger. Frazer will not remember me,— I went to see him in Chelsea, with John Cournos.[3] Charlie Winger, however, will.

You might be able to use some of their drawings.

Yours sincerely,
C. Demuth

TO SCOFIELD THAYER

3 June 1921

Dear Thayer:—

Leo's[4] reported behaviour allows, it would seem, the honour of the province: to rest, as to the great world, on my head.

If you feel sure that money and a canvas of mine can "talk" (I

[1]American writer, editor of *Dial,* and collector of English illustrator Aubrey Beardsley's work. Begun in Chicago in 1880, *Dial* became, under the joint editorship of Thayer and J. Silbey Watson, Jr., the most distinguished literary periodical of the 1920s, printing the work of Sherwood Anderson, Hart Crane, e. e. cummings, T. S. Eliot, D. H. Lawrence, Henry McBride, Thomas Mann, Marianne Moore (who later became its editor when Thayer resigned in 1926 because of mental incapacity), William Carlos Williams, Edmund Wilson, and W. B. Yeats, and reproducing art by Henri Matisse, Pablo Picasso, and many others. The February issue featured Demuth's Precisionist cityscape, *After Sir Christopher Wren,* as frontispiece, about which Henry McBride wrote in his monthly column in the magazine, "Demuth . . . grows in strength if not in gaiety" with "an intensity that suggests an inward rage." Thayer was declared insane in 1930 and spent the last thirty years of his life in a mental institution.

[2]English theater designer.

[3]English-American poet and novelist, whose work had appeared in the "Des Imagistes" issue of *The Glebe,* the little magazine that had printed Demuth's play, *The Azure Adder,* in 1913. Winger has not been identified.

[4]Probably Leo Stein, the brother of Gertrude Stein, noted for his prescience as well as his pedantry in modern art; his collection of Impressionist and Post-Impressionist paintings at the turn of the century in Paris was remarkable.

myself have found them unrelated), at the same pitch,— well then, dear Mr. Thayer, I don't see the way out, and accept your was it "outrageous proposal."[1]

Please make an offer in ready money and write me after looking at the things, remaining from last winter's show, at Daniel's, whichever you would like me to offer on my side. I think that I have no sporting instinct; I feel only, now, in this seeming "almost" crisis that I must support my idea of beauty in the field. It is so much more important for me that it be there, in the field, than on canvas or whatever.

You see you really "got" me. I can't resist doing a canvas on Georges's[2] remembered profile.

Make them show you just what you want to see at Daniel's. You can tell them that your interest is toward the "Dial." Otherwise, knowing the truth, they might wish to protect me. Don't please ask the prices fixed upon them. Now that I'm in, I'll go the handsome with you![3]

Yours sincerely,
C. Demuth

P.S. However, you had better make, at least, two selections. I may be in town before the 2nd which will simplify this sure to be famous bet. Couldn't we have Lloyd's post it?—they might through the McOberon influence.[4]

C. D.

[1]The proposal was for *Dial* to purchase a Demuth painting for its collection.

[2]French pugilist Georges Charpentier.

[3]This now antiquated expression meant to "do the right thing" or "do right by you," but in this case that entailed being disloyal to Charles Daniel, who had featured Demuth's work since 1914.

[4]Lloyd's of London, the celebrated insurance company; McOberon has not been identified.

TO SCOFIELD THAYER
12 June 1921

Dear Thayer:—

Enforced residence in the old home town has made me a bit weak minded perhaps, perhaps careless; more careless, for I believe I am thought to be so by some of my "best" friends, you may have heard as much.

There are two reasons—other than the probable above mentioned—why I accept which I do, you see, gladly, your offer.[1] First you seem to protest a bit over much about my wish in this matter, and, secondly, I hope this act of mine will be the first step in an, anyway, intended row with Mr. Daniel.[2] I wish to get ahold of all my things before I go abroad which will be, with luck, on the 3rd of August.

Are you on your side quite satisfied? I am quite, Mr. Thayer.

I will write Mr. Daniel telling him to hold the one which you have decided upon. I think it is the one used in the "Times." You might go into Daniel and tell him the one, exactly. Tell Hartpence![3]

I will see you before you sail, I hope. If not you, certainly your remarks about Lloyd's.

Yours,
Demuth

I will send you the photographs of the drawings—I think that I have some here; I know Daniel had some. Poor Daniel, art has made him mad. He thought it had a use and tried to find it,— but

[1]Thayer purchased *After Sir Christopher Wren*, 1920.

[2]Demuth was now intent on terminating his association with the Charles Daniel Gallery.

[3]Alanson Hartpence, one of the Imagist poets associated with *Others* and other little magazines of the period, 1913–1919. As proprietor for the Charles Daniel Gallery, he was acquainted with Demuth.

it ain't. Don't tell them at 2 W. 47th St. that I am going to England. C.D.

Can't we have these two in the August "Dial"? Anyway one—[1]

TO SCOFIELD THAYER
postmark 24 June 1921

Dear Thayer:—

About Germany, now that our other matter is arranged!—no, I shall not be going into that, I think, rather nice country. As you see, going into it in Aug. I wish if you go to Berlin you would look up one of my very best friends. He is the one that knows Stefan George,[2] and, I'm sure, many of the other people and things going on in Germany. If you wish I will give you a letter. His address and name are: Arnold Rönnebeck,[3] 3 Offenbacher Str., (Friedsan) Berlin.

I may be in New York next week. I will not see the fight. I couldn't get a seat, a good one when in New York, but now I see that some are to be had. I may see it, but it is not likely. You may slap your neighbor at the fight, Mr. Thayer, when Georges wins.

Did I tell you, Robert Locher[4] is doing a whole production of

[1]Demuth enclosed a newspaper clipping of several photographs of Georges Charpentier and Jack Dempsey, clad in their boxing shorts, in preparation for their upcoming bout.
[2]German expressionist writer.
[3]German sculptor whom Demuth had met at Gertrude Stein's salon, probably through Marsden Hartley. Rönnebeck did a bust of Demuth, now lost, although photographs of it have survived.
[4]American illustrator and designer, Demuth's oldest and most intimate friend; there is no evidence that they were ever lovers. They met circa 1910 and were thereafter in continuous communication. They both contributed to *Rogue,* one of the audacious, prewar little literary magazines. Subsequently, Locher became a leading interior decorator and set and costume designer for theater productions; in part, at least, he may be credited for the popularity of black-and-white Art Deco fashion. During the 1920s, Locher and his wife, Beatrice Howard, lived in France; they returned to the United States and divorced circa 1930. Demuth willed his watercolors to Locher; by Demuth's mother's will, Locher inherited the family house at 118 East King Street in Lancaster.

the new "Greenwich Village Follies."[1] He hopes to come abroad in September and we are planning to be in delicate conditions, for the autumn, somewhere near Nice.

Yours,
Demuth

TO SCOFIELD THAYER
postmark 3 July 1921

Dear Thayer:—

Thanks for the wire. I'm sorry Georges lost, but glad you and "The Dial," in your absence, are to have one of my pictures.[2] I like to think of them being in pleasant places, poor things.

I liked my place between [Benedetto] Croce and [André] Derain; "My place would be between Gilles de Rotz and the Marquis de Sade," wrote [Oscar] Wilde,— too, it is nice being there with Marin[3] to the excluding of all the rest of the painters American.

Give my best wishes to Ezra[4] when you see him,— tell him that I will see him soon, I hope.

My address in London will be "Brown's Hotel," 6 York St., St. James.

Have a good time,— good luck. I shall try again too, at Monte Carlo!

Yours, Demuth

[1]It may have been in the *Greenwich Village Follies* that Demuth first encountered the popular transvestite entertainer Bert Savoy. Henry McBride claimed that Demuth admired Savoy sufficiently to memorialize him in a poster portrait disguised as an oil, *Calla Lilies*. For a reading of this interpretation, see Robin Jaffee Frank, *Charles Demuth: Poster Portraits, 1923–1929* (New Haven: Yale University Press, 1994).

[2]*After Sir Christopher Wren,* 1920; Thayer later gave the painting to the Metropolitan Museum of Art.

[3]American painter John Marin, another of Stieglitz's protégés, whom Demuth admired above all other watercolorists. He was the subject of one of Demuth's "poster portraits."

[4]American modernist poet and critic Ezra Pound.

TO AUGUSTA DEMUTH
postmark 12 August 1921

S.S. Paquebot
Southampton, England

Dear Mother:—

This is Tuesday evening.

We had a very quiet trip.

Miss Sand whom I knew in Etretat the summer that I was there[1] is on the ship, also Mr. Mercer, Mrs. Eshelman's brother.[2]

We will land on Friday. The boat made a very slow run.

I've felt pretty well, the last few days not so well. The food on the ship is getting low. No doubt, I'll be all right when I land.

Bob [Locher] sent me a book. I don't know how it got aboard. Did Beatrice [Locher] meet you? I didn't see her when the boat sailed.

It stayed quite warm all the way over,— not hot though like it had been. To-night it is quite cool. It's too bad you didn't come along. I think that my biscuits will hold out.

I'll write you from London after a day or so. Some one aboard told me of a hotel like the one I stayed at in London before the war. It will be all right, no doubt. It is quite near to the other one.

We've had several dances. And will have one to-night. There were not many people on the ship when it finally sailed, it was about half full.

I hope everything went all right with you. I will write you every week. I suppose things will go all right.

with love,
Charlie

[1]In 1913, Demuth was painting in Etretat, in Normandy.

[2]Brother-in-law of John W. Eshelman, whose family's feed mills served as the model for Demuth's Precisionist oil painting *My Egypt,* 1927.

TO SCOFIELD THAYER
postmark 23 August 1921

Hotel Rembrandt
London, England

Dear Thayer:—

As I said in the wire, Martin[1] was very coy. I didn't really see him, but talked and talked over the phone. My word, it was like twenty tea-parties. He said that they had—the drawing[s]—gone to America. I think that they were really in his trunk. You know how one "gets" these things from the voice, or silences, or whatever. I did all I could,— not much perhaps, but all I could.

He ask[ed] me to send you the [Aubrey] Beardsley book, which I got from John Lane.[2] Martin is sailing to-morrow, Wednesday. I think you will find all the ones on his list, except the "Mlle. de Maupin" one which was only in the first edition, at about forty dollars.

[Demuth's tea spilled on the page at this point so he began a new page, then added his postscripts to the foot of the first page.] I'll try again, as my tea misbehaved.

The Mlle. de M[aupin] looks very nice in the book. She I would have seen there. I'm sure that I would have liked the [*crucial?*] ones the best,— the elephant one first. You must have this one, it can't belong to anyone but you in the land-of-the-free. Do get it.

Martin said that he also had bought some [William] Blakes. They have now at the "Tate" some of great beauty and spirit.

How is Germany? I don't think the man I wanted you to see is in Berlin; Epstein[3] told me that only a few days ago he had a

[1]Probably American antiquarian bookseller Max Martin.
[2]English publisher who founded the Bodley Head publishing house and the influential fin-de-siècle periodical *The Yellow Book*.
[3]English sculptor Jacob Epstein.

card from him from Rome. You may find him returned, however.

I find London quiet, everyone away. Will go to Paris the end of the week or early part of next. My address is Guaranty Trust Co.—London or Paris—how you knew it I don't know. Thanks for the photo of Georges. I received it before I sailed.

If you write,— write to London. I hope you are amused. You owe me 27 shillings, Sir.

Yours,
Demuth

P.S. The tea has dried! If you want the copy of the first edition—"Later Works"—wire me and I'll send it on. It is the last one (?) Mr. Lane has, and was as I said about forty—40.00. Both the clerk at Lane's and Mr. [*Bean?*] seemed to be beyond my control.

P.S. I think the name of my hotel might, if you thought on it, be matter for a last page of some future "Dial."

Demuth

TO ALFRED STIEGLITZ

31 August 1921

Hotel Rembrandt
London, England

Dear Stieglitz:—

You will, no doubt, be surprised to get this from me from this place. It was good to hear from you.

I wanted to do something to stop the "Wheels" going around backwards,— so, chanced this. I wanted so to feel it once more,— so here I am, and will go to Paris next week.

I wish that you were here to look at an exhibition of Blakes, now on at the "Tate," with me. They have been loaned. Some are large pictures on, I think, plaster. They hang next [to] the great Turners—it is wonderful. Marin could be there,— how simple it seems. The National Gallery has been re-arranged by some rare hands,— and one wonderful [El] Greco added.

I wonder if it will ever happen in the land of the free?—or is it happening? I never knew Europe was so wonderful, and never knew really—not so surely—that New York, if not the country, has something not found here. It makes me feel almost like running back and doing something about it,— but what does that come to? So few understand love and work; I think if a few do we may not have lived entirely without point.

You feel the war and what is now going on to an amazing extent. It is all so expressed, so much freer than at home.

Have seen Epstein. His work is really not "there." The sculptors in New York—although I don't get so much—are better. He has become rather grand.

I hope someone opens a gallery in New York. I feel that Daniel is a crook,— a nice fellow, but a crook. I can't cope with it any longer. He had a good chance too. Again the American idea. I have taken most of my things away,— all the good ones. I suppose it was silly but I couldn't come away leaving him to care for them. Poor Stieglitz, some more outside trouble being again poured over you.

I hope your work is going. How grand they looked last winter.

It is more difficult in America to work,— perhaps that will add a quality. My god, where are they? And how little fun they are having.

The enclosed is the new El Greco.

Best regards to G'Kief.

I wish you were here.

Love,
Demuth

TO GERTRUDE STEIN[1]

[circa early September 1921]

Hotel Lutetia, 44 Boulevard Raspail
Paris, France

My dear Miss Stein:—

Could Marsden [Hartley] and I come to see you Saturday evening?

Will you write me to this hotel. I will be here until Mon. or Tues.

Yours sincerely,
Charles Demuth

TO GERTRUDE STEIN

postmark 6 September 1921

Paris, France

Will you be home tomorrow evening,— Wed? Marcel [Duchamp] and I would like to come to see you, if it is all right don't answer, and we will come.

Yours,
Demuth

TO SCOFIELD THAYER

12 September 1921

American Hospital[2]
Neuilly, France

My dear Thayer:—

You will see by the envelope what London and Paris—only a week of Paris—have done for me! No, I think the tea-parties via

[1]Demuth had met Stein during the winter of 1912–1913, when he visited the salon she and Alice B. Toklas held at 27 rue de Fleurus, where he was first exposed to Post-Impressionist and Cubist painting. According to Stein's *The Autobiography of Alice B. Toklas* (New York: Harcourt Brace, 1933), "Demuth . . . was then more interested in writing than in painting."

[2]Apparently Demuth hid from his mother the fact of his hospitalization in France, a period of twelve days, as the result of a combination of too much alcohol and, during his passage abroad, a scarcity of vegetables onboard the ship.

phone with Max [Martin] about the unseen Beardsleys had nothing to do with my present state, and, more or less, enjoyed cure.

I was sorry about the wire, it got to me days after in Paris. You probably are without the book, but Berlin is, after all, the place for information about A[ubrey] B[eardsley]! I don't know, it was all very strange. B—— had certainly made up his mind about my not seeing those drawings. He told me that he had the "Sentimental Education," and then added: "One figure of it, in colour. I think Beardsley cut it in half and coloured the one figure which I have." Again, I don't know. It did look of a stink. I'm sure he had the drawings in his trunk. I would see them certainly before sending the check. He informed [me], with a manner grandly super-salesman, that the price would be high. What did I care? I think on the whole he lacks "tone."

Paris is very beautiful. I think I have never seen it doing so well. I have not seen Ezra [Pound]. I have seen a few of the surrounding English, but Ezra is still to be enjoyed. I think the English friends and,— I was about to add Roedker[1] (a mistake, perhaps) are in the extreme, a tiring lot. They tell me Ezra is still beautiful,— but I never thought that he was. So there we, or they, are.

They seemed, in London, to know nothing about the place to which I wished to wire you. I tried several offices. It was all due to one named Lathrop,[2] from your own dear Mass., that I was able to reach you. He knew of the place which had become mixed in the sending. I think he knows you,— he's from Boston. He has done some "digging" in Mexico, a very nice fellow, trying to be "modern," but still nice. I do feel—but never mind—I feel a great deal at the moment. I'll tell you all about it some other time.

[1]Demuth may be referring to American poet and translator John Roedker or (given his limitations as a speller) John Rodker, English editor and founder of the Ovid Press.

[2]American Tonalist painter William Langstone Lathrop.

Write me from Berlin.

I will stay in Paris or France, I think, through the winter. I may see you. I saw Harold Stearns[1] in London and he whispered of an apartment he was about to have given him in Paris for the winter, so luck, or some "darker lady," no doubt, is still in pursuit. He smelt of gin, but lacked the other charms of the "Beggar's Opera." I am glad I heard it in London—the "Beggar's Opera."[2] I'm surprised it lasted over its opening night in New York. It was so good. Lovat Frazer, the man who did the costumes and set (also for "If" by Lord D[unsanay]) and whom I wanted you to look up, died a few days before I landed in England.

I feel very catty about Martin. I've called him Max above, but I don't care. Max is all right, I'm sure.[3]

Yours—
Demuth

Address: Guaranty Trust Co.
3 rue des Italiens
Paris, Fr.

I love this pen. I haven't written so well in years. Perhaps I'll stop painting. I could make money, paint is very high. I have a lot of gossip. Come to Paris. My style isn't up, at the moment, to the writing of it.

C. D.

[1]American social and cultural historian, associated with *Dial* prior to Thayer and Watson's editorship.

[2]Eighteenth-century ballad opera by John Gay.

[3]Demuth was decorous in adhering to formal address in correspondence and rarely employed first names either directly or in references; alternately, he may have affected the British habit of addressing friends by their surnames.

TO AGNES BOULTON AND EUGENE O'NEILL
17 September 1921

Guaranty Trust Co., 1–2 rue des Italiens
Paris, France

My dear Agie & Eugene:—

I could write as small as you, Eugene, do, with this pen.

Here I am, much to my own and every one's surprise. Marsden [Hartley] is with us,— and really one corner of Paris looks, as to people often seen and always forgotten, like Miss Christine's,[1] or the Brevoort on a ruff night. Marsden seems to love it, having hated the same faces and kind of thing à New York! I can't imagine what of the scenery is left to decorate the Village. Everyone is here, and yet one can be lonely,— must be. Believe me every little piece of "batic"[2] is with us.

However, there are many corners, and Paris is looking the more wonderful, more so really than before the war. And rather cheap living. Joyce is here. I'm going to see him soon with some of the English. His book, part of which came out in the "Little Review," is about to come out, privately printed,— 150 francs if you should want one.[3]

London was very quiet,— but grand, as usual, and unchanged, very expensive, same as New York. It still looks very solid,— but I don't know. The Dunsany thing—I sent you a programme, "If"—was very funny and acted as I have never seen anything acted before for perfection by Violet Cooper and Henry Ainsley. I suppose it will come over,— and fail surely. It's quite good and has had quite a run, in a small theater. Most of the theaters were closed; some, quite a few, were just about to open. There is not

[1]Christine Ell and her husband, Louis.

[2]A reference to batik cloth and similar ethnic and peasant costumery popular in Greenwich Village at the time.

[3]*Ulysses* by James Joyce, which originally appeared in Margaret Anderson's literary journal *Little Review,* was at that time, and until 1933, banned in England and America.

much doing here,— nothing I am told, at the moment, except a small place started by Poiret,[1] L'Oasis.

Marcel [Duchamp] is here and he sent word to me one night before I had seen him to meet him at an address in Montmartre.[2] So I went, he said one o'clock. I got to the place and knocked on the door expecting to enter his apartment, but the door opened only to allow a rolling eye to be seen,— then it opened wide enough to let me in, and I was back on 53rd Street in my favorite cafe, Marshall's. It has moved over complete,— Florence,[3] all. The only thing that is missing is the 6th Ave. El., and the only thing added is a room in which they play "craps." I am waiting to surprise Bobby and Beatrice [Locher]—who are coming next week—with it. It is my high life. I think they only let us in for old time's sake! It looks just like a nigger parlor.[4] I have never on any stage—not even on David's[5]—seen such complete realism. The "moderns," who can afford it are mad about it,— few can. I think Florence has her eye on Marcel or whatever,— so things are cheap for us and they don't make us drink champagne.

[1]French fashion and costume designer Paul Poiret, whose work influenced several American illustrators.

[2]Le Grand Duc, 52 rue Pigalle, a chic black nightclub frequented by American celebrities and tourists.

[3]Florence Embry Jones, an elegant and aloof black entertainer memorialized in three of Demuth's watercolors of black saloon life. Later, she was replaced at Le Grand Duc by Ada Smith, better known as Bricktop. The black restaurant in New York of which Demuth was reminded was in the Marshall Hotel on West Fifty-third Street in the vestiges of New York's "Black Bohemia." Demuth discovered black popular culture and music several years before the subsequently labeled "Harlem Renaissance."

[4]The use of this epithet was common among white people prior to about 1925 and the popular advent of black culture. Black writers did not speak out against its use until then, and it was it was therefore employed more often by whites out of ignorance than out of crudity or malice. There is no evidence in Demuth's correspondence or in accounts of his contemporaries of any conscious racial prejudice, and his watercolors offer palpable evidence of his admiration for black entertainment.

[5]Theatrical entrepreneur David Belasco, notorious for his sumptuous and realistic stage sets.

Elaine[1] wrote that dear old P-town was nice and empty this season and fine. Nice old place,— I love it really. See it next year maybe. I'll probably stay over through the winter, or come back at Christmas time with Robert [Locher] and wife. I am certainly looking forward to next week. I haven't gone about much here, as yet, being none too well, damn it, but will start, I hope, or be able to, on their arrival. We're all so thin now, the three of us,— everything stops to look. Hope you are well.

love,
Demuth

TO AUGUSTA DEMUTH
postmark 29 September 1921

Paris, France

[Robert Locher wrote this postcard, to which Demuth added a postscript. "We have enjoyed a busy week in Paris and are leaving for the South to-morrow. Susan Street[2] joined us here at Charles Hotel and we've been having a regular house party. Charles is very well and is very comfortable here. The weather has been wonderful. Will be back here in 2 weeks. Hoping you are well, with love, Bobby and Bea."]

Am all right and will write you to-morrow.

love,
Charlie

[1]Elaine Freeman, the Provincetown roommate of Helene Iungerich, on whom Demuth "had a kind of a crush," according to American painter Stuart Davis—though it seems to have been an artistic infatuation rather than a romantic one. Demuth's name has also been linked romantically but vaguely with Polly Holladay and Emmasita Register, though there no evidence he was involved romantically with either. He seems to have genuinely enjoyed the social or artistic companionship of several women, including Georgia O'Keeffe, all three Stettheimer sisters, Helen Henderson, Susan Street, Elsie Everts, and Agnes Boulton O'Neill.

[2]Susan Watt Street, an American friend of Demuth's and a collector of his work, with Provincetown connections.

TO SCOFIELD THAYER

2 October 1921

Paris

Dear Thayer:—

I am glad that in my name you "sat on" Martin. It makes me feel like a "power" in the world of art and business. I am glad that you got a good Beardsley à Berlin. Robert Locher who is now with me, knows the one which you have recently bought, and tells me that, from the book, it looks, to him, very fine.

He and Mrs. Locher came over about ten days ago. They are now in the South but will come back to me and Paris in a week or two. We, I think, will stay on through the winter.

I have hear[d] from Berlin and your visit. I am glad, so very glad, really, that you found Arnold [Rönnebeck], and that you liked some of his things and my head. I must have one done in bronze, I think.[1] Maybe I'll go to Berlin and have a look at it. I had almost forgotten it. Marsden [Hartley] goes to Berlin in about three weeks,— may do it with him. Perhaps the "Dial" would like one to stand on the mantel over which hangs the "Jack-Georges" Demuth.[2]

I have found a beautiful [Henri de Toulouse-]Lautrec. You will like it, I think.

As you see,— I mean, by the violet of the paper, I have left the hospital (inc.). And am going more or less "merrily," as you wished, once more.

[1]Demuth refers here to photographs of Rönnebeck's bust portrait of him, probably made in Berlin in 1913.

[2]Demuth executed two paintings of boxers, one of which has not survived; he may only be referring to Thayer's painting, *After Sir Christopher Wren,* labeling it with the kind of fanciful or private title he sometimes gave his work, in this case because of his earlier references to the Dempsey-Charpentier prizefight.

Are you staying on in odd out-of-the-way, but less expensive places, or are you going to England. I will send this to London.

Hoping you find many pretty pictures and other forms of art.

Yours,
Demuth

TO GERTRUDE STEIN
[circa early October 1921]

Hotel Lutetia
Paris, France

My dear Miss Stein:—

Could we see you to-morrow night? There are two friends of mine in Paris who have a letter to you from C. Van Vechten.[1]

We came to see you last week. If all right don't answer—otherwise Hotel Lutetia.

Demuth

TO ALFRED STIEGLITZ
10 October 1921

Paris, France

Dear Stieglitz:—

I wish that you were here. Indeed you should be here. Of course, there is your work which is first. But there is a great need at the moment for you, here.

All the French painters, the great ones, and the men interested in the two magazines,— "L'Amour de l'Art" and "L'Esprit Nouveau," are very anxious to have the best of the Americans in with them. It is a thrill, really, to hear what they think of us, knowing us so slightly,

[1]American music critic and novelist Carl Van Vechten, an early (1922) Demuth supporter, and Stein's most persistent advocate in America. The friends referred to are Beatrice and Robert Locher. Van Vechten probably met Demuth through Locher when they were all contributing to *Rogue*, circa 1915, or through the Arensbergs.

mostly through the "Dial,"—strange, isn't it?—but it is thought very well of in France & England. I am told either of the Rosenbergs[1] will have our things,— and they have very impressive galleries. All the moderns are shown with great spirit—and there is no showing of the old masters as an excuse for their being,— the spirit of often showing the younger men only to sell a Lawson[2] is lacking entirely!

Pach[3] who was here, as he is everywhere, was asked to do an article and, of course, did. But it will not be used—they were more "on" than Pach thought. There is no one to do it in French and, really, one should be done at once,— they are so anxious and willing. Pach left everyone out—Marin, Weber,[4] Sheeler,[5] G'Kieff—everyone. But as I said the French were more "on" than he knew. It would be so grand to be taken up, en masse, by the French, who know a "bit" about painting, after the way the mother country has treated us,— wouldn't it? So you see you really should be here. Of course, I can do something, I hope. The Pach thing has been stopped anyway.

Pound has done a lot, but he really doesn't know about painting. It is all very amazing to me to find this enthusiasm, here,— after knowing what we have always felt for the French, not thinking much of our own; and the great Frenchmen telling us that we are very good. It seems rather grand. It is like Baudelaire and Poe. I wish that you could be here to get the thrill of it,— after the work and love you have given the painters French & American. It seems almost as though the dream were "coming true,"— that after all art is not <u>only</u> pictures, books, etc.,— but also the nearest

[1]Paul and Leonce Rosenberg had galleries in both New York and in Paris.

[2]American painter Ernest Lawson, some of whose paintings Charles Daniel accepted to cover a bar bill; Daniel represented at various times not only Demuth but Marsden Hartley, John Marin, and others of their generation.

[3]American art critic Walter Pach, an advisor and go-between for galleries in Paris and New York.

[4]American painter Max Weber.

[5]American painter Charles Sheeler, also represented by the Charles Daniel Gallery.

we can get to,— you can call it what you like,— I'll write, Sympathetic Order!

Paris is as you see rather wonderful. It seems to shine. One feels, perhaps, it is the last grand flair. I don't know,— it seems almost too grand.

I think that I will stay on for another month or two,— and then come home. Had I stayed when I first came over—I was only twenty[1]—well, I might have gotten into it. Now it would take years,— and work would seem so only on the surface of the scene during that time. I feel "In" America—even though its insides are empty. Maybe I can help fill them. It would be so easy to stay. Strange that I should feel this; I don't think it has shown yet in my work. Maybe it never will, however—

I heard from Barnes,— his part in the Metropolitan fight.[2] It seems almost impossible. Hear the very new men are almost old masters—the world is almost ready for another turn—and New York two, at least, turns behind. Sometimes it seems almost impossible to come back,— we are so out of it. Then one sees Marcel [Duchamp] or Gleizes,[3] and they will say, "Oh! Paris. New York is the place,— there are the modern ideas. Europe is finished." How wonderful a time it is. I'm glad, missing the

[1]Demuth first went to Europe in 1907, when he was twenty-four. See his 17 September 1907 letter to William Carlos Williams and his 13 November 1922 letter to Gilbert Seldes.

[2]American patent magnate Dr. Albert C. Barnes, who amassed what is arguably the finest private collection of modern art in the world, including many Demuths, and created his own institution for the study of art, in Merion, Pennsylvania, a suburb north of Philadelphia. When the Metropolitan Museum of Art mounted an exhibition of modernist paintings, an anonymous pamphlet was circulated quoting Francis Dercum, a Philadelphia physician who had condemned modern painters as "insane" during a speech before the Philadelphia Art Alliance in April 1921. Barnes rose to the defense of the Metropolitan, offering to contribute his entire collection to Philadelphia, and build a gallery to house it, if Dercum could prove himself qualified to make such judgments. When Dercum ignored the challenge, Barnes then offered to build a museum to house the works of modernist painter John Johnson. Dercum demurred.

[3]French painter Albert Gleizes, who emigrated in 1915, arriving to declare the Brooklyn Bridge a work of art to rival Notre Dame de Paris.

Renaissance (I suppose that I did!), that I was not called upon to live at any other time,— aren't you?

Hartley is going to Berlin in a week or two. After Xmas he expects to go to Rome with Rönnebeck who is to have a class there. He may help. Germany is having an "inning" in Italy at the moment.

Saw Gertrude Stein. She is fat and handsome and rides in the smallest "Ford" Henry ever turned out,— also the most ugly. She is rather grand. But unlike the French thinks that we are all very dull. I do think she should have a few months in the home land. I took some friends of mine [Robert and Beatrice Locher] to see her,— and she liked them, and then asked me on the quiet if they really hadn't been over here for a long time. They didn't seem of the dullness she expected. I suppose in 17 years things have changed.

So you see where we are at,— or maybe where we are not. I wish you were here.

Best regards for G'Kieff,— and, too, for you.

Yours,
Demuth

TO AUGUSTA DEMUTH
12 October 1921

Paris, France

Paris is just the same. How are your flowers,— have you moved them all?[1]

Charlie

[1]Augusta Demuth's extensive gardens behind the family home were laid out in eighteenth-century patterns, with formally patterned brick walks among them. Their annual bounty was frequently subject matter for Demuth's watercolors.

TO WILLIAM CARLOS WILLIAMS
13 October 1921

Paris

Dear Carlos:—

I thought that you might like this little book, on Matisse.[1]

It is generally reported here, and in London, that you are our only poet,— living, of course, cher Carlos.

France thinks a great deal of our art. Of course, it all seems strange, never knowing we had one!

Paris is more wonderful than ever,— but I must hurry back to Lancaster and work. I'm too old to stay.

Love,
Demuth

TO AUGUSTA DEMUTH
15 October 1921

Paris, France

Dear Mother:—

Your latest letters, the two with the four-leaved clovers, have been received. I hope with you that they bring me luck.

Bob [Locher], who got back from the South to-day, says that I'm looking, he thinks, as when I was well. I'm not quite that fat, as yet, but do look and feel pretty well.

Beatrice was quite ill in the South,— and looks none too well, poor thing. She has something wrong with her stomach and must go on a diet, but not the same as mine.

For the last two days it has been cool here, and we feel that may be the summer is over.

Bob says that he has sent you cards from the South. It must be very lovely.

[1]Charles Vildrac, *Cinquanate dessins par Henri-Matisse* (Paris, 1920).

Sue [Street] has taken a nice apartment,— I saw it to-day. They will be very comfortable in it, I think. And it will be very nice for them indeed. Bob says that Lila and Segar[1] are in Cleveland, so that leaves their house with no one in it. He says that I should tell you to come over, that we all need you. You might like it.

I think you can count on me coming home about the 30th of November, that is leaving here about that time.

One of the galleries in Paris [Leonce Rosenberg] has taken my things, a quite good place. Of course I only had one or two things which I have done here, still it will be an opening if I ever want to come back, or send things over here. They liked my things.

In lots of ways I would like to stay, but I think I've been lucky to get three or four months the way things are at present.

A lot of people are going to Germany. Arnold Rönnebeck writes that I should come up with Hartley, but I don't think that I will this time. I would love to go, but it is rather a long trip, and I get tired carrying bread and stuff around Europe. No, I suppose I won't go, or try to go to Italy,— I thought that I would maybe.

I'm glad that the flowers did so well. They are all doing very well still, here. The gardens look fine and gay, although it never seems to rain. Other times I've been here it was raining all the time, now it never rains.

If you send me Mrs. McKnight's address I will send her a card[2] I sent the others which you wanted me to send, last week.

Paris is livening up for the winter. The picture exhibitions are starting and the theaters are opening with new plays. I went to the opera last week, it was quite grand, but ours is really better.

[1]Robert Locher's sister, Lila, and her husband, Roland Segar. After Segar's death she married Brian Swan; their daughter was responsible for depositing some of Richard Weyand's materials about Demuth's life and work at Yale University. Some members of Weyand's family deposited material as well.

[2]Julia McKnight, a neighbor who lived at 201 East King Street in Lancaster.

I hope you are all right—don't get too excited over the autumn house cleaning!

Lovingly,
Charlie

TO GERTRUDE STEIN
[circa mid-October 1921]

Paris, France

My dear Gertrude Stein:—

It will be all right for me, Wed. evening. Thanks, would love to. The Lochers are coming back Sunday.

Yours,
Demuth

TO AUGUSTA DEMUTH
17 October 1921

Paris, France

Dear Mother:—

Your letter with the photos just came, and, as I was writing to Barnes, about a picture that he wishes me to buy for him,[1] I thought that I would write you just a short letter too.

I think the pictures quite good of you and Ida[2] and the moon-flower!— and was glad to hear that the Kauffmans[3] were with you.

Now that Bob [Locher] is back I see him almost every day,— and that makes it nice.

I write to Barnes quite often. I'll be nice to him,— I like him and he has been nice to me.

[1]*Issey le Moulineaus,* 1919, by Henri Matisse.

[2]Mrs. Christopher Demuth, née Smith, Demuth's father's sister-in-law.

[3]Unidentified family friends; Kauffman was and still is an extremely common name in Lancaster.

If I need any money, I'll let you know. We can fix about the watch when I get back. The way things look my money would hold out until about March. Of course, if I come back at the end of Nov. I'll still have some. I haven't gotten passage but will in a week or so if I decide to come back.

I've put all the four leaved clovers in my shoes. I've been quite well for a week or ten days,— hoping you are, with love—

Lovingly,
Charlie

TO AUGUSTA DEMUTH
postmark 17 October 1921

Paris, France

Writing these while I wait for him—I had a letter from Barnes— he is doing over the house, the up-stairs.[1] Sent Aunt Kate[2] a card for birthday, will write in a few days—

Love,
Charlie

TO AUGUSTA DEMUTH
[circa October 1921]

Paris, France

Didn't get any letter from you this week, but I didn't either get any other American mail, so maybe there were no boats. Am all right, have made no arrangements about sailing. Will cable you,— it will be [*during?*] November sometime.

C.

[1]In Merion, Pennsylvania.
[2]Catherine Buckius, Augusta Demuth's sister.

TO AUGUSTA DEMUTH

7 November 1921

Paris, France

Dear Mother:—

My lovely birthday present came a day or two ago. It was a little early, as this is Monday the 7th, as I write, and to-morrow will be my birthday. Still as you say the boats are now fewer, and I did get it. Thank you, very much. I gave Bob [Locher] what you wanted him to have. I gave it to him at once, as they are rather hard up, on account of some money still owed him from the theater job of the past summer.

The bread and cakes I get here are very good, not as good maybe as those in London, but all right. The other things, vegetables, I [am] afraid have some things in them some times which do not agree with me. I don't know, most of the time I've been pretty well, but I've gotten very little fatter. But I look about the same really.

I've decided to come home on the Paris sailing next Saturday—that will be the 12th of Nov.—and will land on the 19th, I hope. I will cable you to-day and, I hope, that you get this letter a few days before the 19th, but I'm afraid that there are few boats sailing before the Paris, so this may cross with me.

All together it has been a nice trip, and lasted longer than I expected, really. I thought that I had better come home now, than nearer Christmas, as I did not expect to stay on over Christmas.

If you want to meet me, all right. The boat lands on a Saturday if it is on time. We can stay in New York over Sunday. If you don't want to come, and I don't find you at the dock, I'll call you up at once from New York.

Bob is doing some work for Poiret. It may lead to a good job. He has just started to work and we don't know what money will be in it for him. But it will be something to have worked with Poiret while here. They think that they will stay until the New Year. Beatrice is feeling better.

In a week or two, now, I can tell you all about my trip.

I will not bother about the bag for Christopher [Demuth]. I would not travel around with it and it would look brand new, and there would be duty. And I have my clothes, and a few things and I don't want any more stuff to make the list longer. I've gotten something for Ida. And the muffler for Christopher.

The trunks and things like that are almost as expensive as they are at home,— and no better.

Hoping you get this before the boat lands, and to see you soon. Don't worry, I'm really all right,— or almost, and with love, believe me.

Lovingly,
Charlie

TO ALFRED STIEGLITZ
28 November 1921

Dear Stieglitz:—

You made a good guess.— the letter found me at home,— two days at home. Your letter made me glad to be home, and I will see you soon in New York.

It was all very wonderful,— but I must work, here. Had I stayed in France when I went to it for the first time,— by now I would be into it. It would take years, and after all there are many able Frenchmen,— and New York is something which Europe is not,— and I feel of that something—awful, as most of it is. Marcel [Duchamp] and all the others, those who count, say that all the "modern" is to us, and of course they are right, but it is so hard.

The Autumn Salon was dead,— about five years dead. Braque seemed to be growing in quality—they are quite lovely—and Marcel, dear Marcel, is doing some wonderful "movies." Picasso is doing, and doing, and doing. He has a new wife, a real wife[1],—that is, she is getting him away from all his old friends. There is a great deal to tell you of Europe. Marcel seems to be the only one really working.

At the moment I feel that I wish to grow fast,— even to Lancaster. I am so tired. Maybe it is my health, but I suspect it is more from hearing so often, "I must go to Berlin, or Rome, or Vienna, or Florence, or the East, or the South Seas. I know there must be something there for <u>me.</u>" I so often wished at hearing them that some would, or all would, go to hell.

What work I do will be done here; terrible as it is to work in this "our land of the free."

We will talk it out together, soon. I could write a book about it, of course, but all that is left of my energy, I suspect, had better go into painting!

Together we will add to the American scene, more than has been added since the 60's and 70's,— maybe more than they added. I feel that all together we are more or less fine. I want to see New York for three or four months, maybe after the New Year.

Love to you and G'Kieffe,
Demuth

P.S. If you are able send me the Hartley book.[2] He is in Berlin.

C.D.

[1]Picasso had married Russian ballet dancer Olga Koklova in July 1918.

[2]Marsden Hartley, *Adventures in the Arts: Informal Chapters on Painters, Vaudeville, and Poets,* with an introduction by Waldo Frank (New York: Boni and Liveright, 1921). Frank was a well-known American novelist and critic who combined poetic mysticism and political liberalism.

TO GERTRUDE STEIN

[circa December 1921]

Wishing you and Miss Toclas[1] a Merry Xmas and a Happy New Year.

Write me just what those Civil War pictures are called and the publisher and I'll look it up for you.

Yours,
Demuth

TO A. E. GALLATIN[2]

8 February 1922

My dear Mr. Gallatin:—

Your note was received to-day.

You say that I may look you up when in town, which is rather often, I think it would be easier than writing you the information.[3] I would like to see your collection.

It was nice to know that my two water-colours which you now own,[4] will be with the Marins,— Marin, whom I think the greatest water-colourist of our time.

I will phone you when next in town, which will be towards the end of Feb.

Yours sincerely,
C. Demuth

[1]Friends and strangers alike misspelled Alice B. Toklas's name in a variety of ways, even over a period of years; Stein never made any effort to correct this.

[2]American art critic, painter, and collector, the author of several books, including *American Water-Colourists* (New York: E. P. Dutton, 1922) and *Charles Demuth* (New York: William Edwin Rudge, 1927). Gallatin was one of Demuth's earliest enthusiasts. He established the Gallery of Living Art, now a permanent collection at New York University.

[3]Gallatin was collecting information from the subjects to be included in his *American Water-Colourists.*

[4]*In Vaudeville,* 1918, and *Zinnias,* 1921.

TO ALFRED STIEGLITZ

19 February 1922

Dear Stieglitz:—

Will you arrange about the price of my things?—please.

And will you drop me a card; how are the pictures to be sold, in what order. Will it go by the alphabet? If it does I would like, maybe, to bid on some things.[1] Will you write me. I may come over.

Barnes is in Florida,— so will not be at the sale. You might let Sam White[2] know, but I don't have his address.

Good luck. I hope I see you Thursday.

Yours,
Demuth

TO CARL VAN VECHTEN

postmark 26 March 1922

Hotel Brevoort, Fifth Avenue at 8th Street
New York City

Dear Carl:—

I had to wait until I reached the capital, and, en route to a "rest cure," before I could write you about the "flower" article.[3]

Your very frisky and urbane lines about me made me wish that

[1]Stieglitz mounted an auction of paintings at the Anderson Galleries, all chosen by the artists, according to a note in the *New York Times,* 22 February 1922. The anonymous author of "Art Notes" said that Stieglitz had mounted this as "a sporting event" and dismissed most of the work as inferior, but he conceded that "Charles Demuth has refinement of drawing and beauty of color and sends them both to this auction in his ragged yellow flowers against airy gray shadows." Probably this referred to *Mixed Flowers,* 1917. Hartley, Fisk, and Sheeler were among the few others to whose work the *Times* writer gave grudging praise. The rest of paintings he dismissed as inferior.

[2]Philadelphia art collector and dental equipment manufacturer Samuel S. White.

[3]"Charles Demuth and Florine Stettheimer," one of Van Vechten's "Pastiches et Pistaches," a series of brief essays published in *The Reviewer,* February 1922, one of the earliest appreciations of their paintings to appear in print.

I could really be as naughty as you imagine; perhaps I can be after the "cure," dear Carl.[1]

The article was very sympathetic, and unlike most did not rest on the words "Beauty" and "Art." Thanks.

Yours,
Demuth

P.S. I looked that matter up of which you spoke,— W[aldo] F[rank]'s closing lines in his introduction to Mr. Hartley's book on "Art."[2] That's where seriousness about art can land one.

TO WILLIAM CARLOS WILLIAMS
9 June 1922

Box 308
Morristown, New Jersey

Cher Carlos:—

We had such a nice ride over.

Don't worry,— it is all, all right.[3] What you want is only what we all want only in this part of the scene. There isn't really very much, if any, of "That."

Do take the month abroad. It is almost enough,— really quite.

Am sending you the poems of Emily Dickinson. What a treat,— there was a girl, the biggest New Englander of them all.

Love, dear boy,
Charlie

[1]The following month, Demuth committed himself for treatment under the care of Frederick Allen, M.D., at the Physiatric Institute in Morristown, New Jersey, formerly the private residence of theatrical producer Otto Kahn and built in terra cotta imitation of the Versailles Palace.

[2]See page 38, footnote 2.

[3]Demuth was first treated through a starvation diet—carefully measured amounts of food. He was able to work now and then; his mother sent him flowers regularly from her garden; Alfred C. Barnes helped finance his stay; Robert Locher brought him a then banned copy of James Joyce's *Ulysses,* all of which must have contributed to his feeling that "it is all, all right."

TO ALFRED STIEGLITZ
30 July 1922

Box 308
Morristown, New Jersey

Dearest Stieglitz:—

Just a line, in the heat and,— in other things as trying, to tell you that I don't have Hartley's address,— have not had a line since we parted in Paris,— you know Marsden. I thought that his "page" in V.F.[1] was,— looked very splendid; it was fine.

I'm working a bit. My old age has started,— at least Middle period! It's great fun. Am enclosing—I think—a very good report of myself (and garden) in July 1922. Hope you like it. Sorry couldn't do something for "MSS." about camera.[2] Couldn't,— very little left after I do my daily (sometimes, now weekly) painting.

Love, to both,
Demuth

TO A. E. GALLATIN
11 September 1922

My dear Mr. Gallatin:—

When I saw you in the spring, you said that in the autumn you might be interested in seeing some of my "vaudeville" drawings and water-colours of architectural forms. Are you still interested? If you are, I will send you a selection which you could look over. I am rather in need of selling at the moment; perhaps we could arrange something pleasant for us both.

[1]"The Paintings of Marsden Hartley" by Paul Rosenfeld, with four illustrations, *Vanity Fair,* July 1922.

[2]Stieglitz, planning a new issue of his periodical, *Manuscripts,* asked Demuth to write something in reply to the question, "Can a photograph have the significance of art?" In the photograph Demuth enclosed with his reply, he is alarmingly thin from the dietary treatments he had been undergoing at the Physiatric Institute.

Hoping to hear that you are still interested and that you have had a nice summer, I remain,

Yours sincerely,
C. Demuth

TO WILLIAM CARLOS WILLIAMS
16 October 1922

[telegram]
Lancaster, Pennsylvania

FORGIVE LONG SILENCE[1] LOVE

DEMUTH

TO GILBERT SELDES[2]
13 November 1922

My dear Seldes:—

Please pardon me,— I just forgot it, really I did, and I don't understand it, as I'm as anxious as the best of "them," towards fame (so called) or publicity.

Here goes: I was born Nov 8th 1883, studied at the Pennsylvania Academy of the Fine Arts under William M[erritt] Chase and Thomas Anshutz. I went to Paris in 1907 for the first time and afterwards returned to it in 1912 and in 1921, living there and in London during these visits, about four years in all.

I have exhibited at the Penna. Academy and at the Daniel Gallery in New York City.

[1]Demuth had been in the sanatorium in Morristown for most of the summer. These recuperative dietary sessions were apparently emotionally as well as physically debilitating.
[2]American cultural critic, best known for his cultural history of the postwar period, *The Seven Lively Arts* (1924); at this time he was one of the editors of *Dial*.

I think this is about the limit of my knowledge about myself. I suppose you will answer: "Know thyself, young man."

Sincerely,
Demuth

P.S. I hope that I will see you before you go abroad. I would like to see you. Perhaps with great luck we can do the 14th St place,— and then the "Palace."[1] That would be a nice evening.

Remember me to dear Scofield [Thayer] when you write. I hope he hurries back,— he amuses. Yours, C. D.

TO A. E. GALLATIN

postmark [date indecipherable] 1922

My dear Mr. Gallatin:—

The book[2] was in Lancaster and was not forwarded to me, when I returned Monday, having been away for some weeks.[3] I found it and on opening it had my great pleasure.

The book is very beautiful, and, too, very flattering. But really it is beautiful. It was very kind of you to send it me and someday you must sign it. Thank you very much.

I will look you up when in New York. I only had a few hours this time, but would have called you but was told that recently you had the sad experience of the death of your mother. Accept, please, my sympathy.

[1]Demuth frequently attended vaudeville performances at the Palace Theatre, always when the transvestite entertainer Bert Savoy was playing. Both Demuth and Seldes admired Savoy and memorialized him in their work: Seldes in reviews and Demuth ostensibly in a "poster portrait," *Calla Lilies*. See page 16, footnote 1.

[2]*American Water-Colourists* by Gallatin, which contained an appreciation of Demuth and reproductions of his work.

[3]Weakness had forced Demuth back to the Physiatric Institute in late November. Although insulin was then available, Demuth did not agree to avail himself of it for nearly a year.

Perhaps after the New Year we can have some hours, hours which were on my spring visit to your house so charming.

I hope the new year and the holidays will bring you joy.

Yours sincerely,
Demuth

TO ALFRED STIEGLITZ
December 1922

Wishing you & G'Kief Merry holidays, and a great coming year—'23—it contains one of "our" numbers!

Charles Demuth

TO ALFRED STIEGLITZ
10 January 1923

Dearest Stieglitz:—

Have sent you the water-colours, as you ask[ed] me to do, after the show.[1] The one of the egg-plant and the two of the cyclamen you have not before seen.

Let me know when G'Kiefe will show her things, if she does this season.

The Carles[2] show was nice, I thought, the room was gay—sweetly Matisse—but all right.

Remember me to Duncan[3] & Dove,[4] and G'Kief.

[1]Following this exhibition at Charles Daniel's gallery, Ferdinand Howald purchased three Demuth paintings, one for $550, two for $500 each: *Tower,* 1920; *Incense of a New Church,* 1921; *Paquebot "Paris,"* 1921–1922. Demuth, who was then returning to the Morristown sanatorium for diabetic treatments, would be "relieved for a while," Daniel wrote to Howald. Howald later gave all three paintings to the Columbus (Ohio) Museum of Art.
[2]American artist Arthur B. Carles, a Philadelphia friend from Demuth's early days there.
[3]American artist Charles Duncan, of whom Demuth painted a poster portrait.
[4]American artist Arthur Dove, of whom Demuth painted a poster portrait.

Will, I hope, see you soon.

Am trying to write something about Washington Allston for the "Arts,"[1] and I'm painting a little.

Love,
Demuth

TO ALFRED STIEGLITZ
29? January 1923

Dear Stieglitz:—

Will you be terribly up-set if I say that you & G'K. may have them and must not go to Hell; not yet, as I'm still hanging onto this world, and don't want you to be in a sphere where I am not.

I do want you to have the water-colours, and, as Daniel has sold one or two,— well below the "thousands," however, what you offer me will be o.k. between us. I'd rather you'd have them than Warren G. Harding or the Museum at 5th and 81st![2]

I will try to come for G'K's first day—the 29th—it is my mother's birthday.[3]

Perhaps you can do my hands then. That will be wonderful if you would. It, if you wish to do them, would, I feel, be well to do them soon, for in the language of the moment: Every day they grow thinner and thinner.[4]

[1]Demuth was especially enthusiastic about this eighteenth-century artist but nothing he may have written about him has survived. Allston was perhaps the first American painter to clarify the difference between artisan and artist. He was a writer as well, and widely recognized for his personal elegance and style. Also, as if in anticipation of Demuth, Allston painted in several styles.

[2]Both the current president of the United States and the Metropolitan Museum of Art represented authority and control.

[3]Demuth refers here to an exhibition of O'Keeffe's current work at Stieglitz's gallery.

[4]Many people who knew Demuth commented on his expressive hands and elongated fingers, with which he frequently gesticulated. Either he asked Stieglitz or Stieglitz asked him to photograph them.

I'm glad you want the egg-plant. I kept it here; it turned into a heart,— maybe mine; anyway I hope no one will discover "Art" or "Painting" engraved on it.

Good luck for the show,— & love. Will see you when in town, at Anderson [Art Galleries], or will call you if I don't find you there,— as soon as I get in so we can arrange about photo of hands.

Yours,
Demuth

TO AGNES AND EUGENE O'NEILL
[circa 10 February 1923]

Dear Agnes & Eugene:—

I am answering promptly, why God knows—I have little to write, or tell. I feel these days that we have more or less said everything to each other. I would love to be able to sit on your beach and look at you and be near you in almost silence. This sounds like love,— sweet Plato—I at times near Nirvana—great health, as Miss Paula[1] once said, is greatly overrated. I believe that it is, as a giver of repose, surely.

The "photo" was very nice. It is nice to have a private one. I mean there are so many public ones these days of Eugene and yourself! Look up "Sudden-Land" next month. One of mine will be given to the "World." I wanted them to use Charles among his flowers, which I sent you, but they couldn't see it,— of course they couldn't,— that was too much to expect.

I don't suppose that I will get to P[rovince]-town. this year, but plan to do so early next, with Mother,— we'll get a house. It

[1]Paula Holladay (or Holliday), better known as "Polly," operated a series of popular Greenwich Village restaurants, the first with her chef and lover, the Russian anarchist Hippolyte Havel, in the basement of the Liberal Club on MacDougal Street, next-door to the Provincetown Playhouse. She later opened a succession of other restaurants though none rivaled the first in popularity and notoriety.

got too late this year. I love it there, and it seems to be growing less popular, which will be too wonderful, if true. What it had is so rare. A foggy night in that sea-village,— oh, baby,— for depression, not even gin in London can compare. I've loved it,— well, I have loved several things well,— the "paper of proof,"— my "photo" among my flowers,— but it was a grand 38 years,— it was Kitty, it was!

When will you be in town,— and what of the winter? Do you go to Italy? I go to New York about once a month, to see Robert [Locher] and Daniel and sometimes the doctor. I may be there for two or three months in the new year. My work goes on rather well, here, at present.

10 February 1923

Second part—first being in answer to the summer's letter with 'photo.

Thanks, dear Agie, for the book, which I didn't have but wanted. It was so nice of you, old dear,— there are some great things in that book.

How is the new estate in Vt.,— is it. Do give me an address.

May be in New York soon. I don't know. Where is Eddy [Fisk]? And what are they up to? Give him my love. And what are you & Eugene up to?

Do, if you haven't, read the "Song of Maladore," it was in four numbers of the "Broom."[1] There was madness, the real kind,— to think we were really not after all mad enough. What a disappointment!

Thanks, Agie, and love to you & Eugene.

Demuth

[1]"The Lay of Maladore" by Isadore Ducasse, Comte de Lautréamont, translated by Demuth's friend John Roedker, ran in *Broom,* August to December 1922 (five installments).

TO A. E. GALLATIN
postmark 26 February 1923

My dear Mr. Gallatin:—

I received your very nice letter some time ago. I was glad to know that you got the flowers and the vaudeville thing.

This past week I sent you by p[arcel] p[ost] a few vaudeville things—all I have in fact, of this past "period." If you do not like any of them you can return them to me here. I have no "factory" ones. There will be *[two missing words]* perhaps your letter, the part about your walks in the park, makes me want to do some more along these lines,— it was fine; so seldom does one get just that from people.

I hope that I see you soon. I am not very well and can not very easily get away from my province.

Did you see the page of beauties in V.F. of this month![1] We are not up to the pages of aviators, or musicians, which Mr. Frank Crowninshield sometimes uses!

Very sincerely yours,
Demuth

TO A. E. GALLATIN
6 March 1923

My dear Mr. Gallatin:—

The drawings, which you returned to me, arrived.

I am quite satisfied about the one you liked, & like to think of them with your Marins,— on that wall. Probably this one will not

[1]A full page of photographs of contemporary painters—Demuth, Duchamp, Hartley, Sheeler, Marin, Joseph Stella, Max Weber, and William Zorach—in *Vanity Fair,* March 1923, edited by Frank Crowninshield. About Demuth: "He is never heavy-handed or obvious; his art has wit, piquancy, cultivation and an original outlook. The artist should supply us with a new vision. This Demuth has done."

go on that wall.[1] Still—some of mine are there. The light is so fine for water-colours. It would be fine and I should so love it,—the having you put me up. I will call you up when in town, if my whatever it is will allow it.

Hoping to see you soon,

Sincerely,
C. Demuth

TO ALFRED STIEGLITZ
12 March 1923

Dearest Stieglitz:—

Could you take those drawings: water-colours—which you brought to Of's[2]— some time before Thurs? I'll be in town Thurs. and Fri. I'll clean them up at Of's and select some molding for the frames,— something white and very simple. In the general excitement that day we forgot about the frames.

Am going to Morristown[3] Fri. Will see you at the Marin show.

Have two more water-colours which if you do not mind I will leave at Of's. You can look at them and if you would like to have them for a while I would be glad. [Daniel's gallery at] 2 W. 47 is so awful these days.

We can arrange, however, when I see you later in week.

Yours,
Demuth

P.S. I have written and talked to Barnes—I hope to some end—but god knows about the Marins. I think that he will be in. Don't,

[1]Probably Demuth's illustration for Émile Zola's *L'Assommoir,* 1918.

[2]American painter and professional framer George Of.

[3]Stieglitz was aware of Demuth's periodic trips to the Physiatric Institute for rest and recuperation because of his diabetes; Demuth first received insulin injections during this stay.

if you can prevent [it], have Montross[1] fuss over him. I think this might help a possible sale. I hope that he takes those sea things. They are the only really great marines since [Gustav] Courbet,— I think. [Winslow] Homer's, after all, were illustrations—of course, really good illustrations, but still only that. Martin[2] and Marin will be some day a great vogue,— Martin, almost at this late day (for him), almost as unknown as Marin is.

Demuth

TO A. E. GALLATIN
postmark 26 March 1923

Box 308
Morristown, New Jersey

My dear Mr. Gallatin:—

As you will see I am at Morristown, again.

I did not unpack the drawings, nor did I read your letter, it seems, very carefully.

If you want the drawing I will have it sent me, here; I mean, if you want it at once, otherwise if you could wait I will sign it at once on my return and send it you. I may be here two or three weeks. If my mother comes to see me I will have her bring it along.

I am sorry,— but was not very well at the time, and things, I see, have gotten a bit mixed.

However, the drawing is safe.

Yours,
C. Demuth

[1]Imperious and snobbish art dealer Newman E. Montross, who capitalized as early as 1914 on the new popularity for modern American painting.
[2]American Tonalist painter Homer Dodge Martin.

[Demuth next wrote to Gallatin on two postcards, each with the same postmark, carrying his message from one to the other.]

TO A. E. GALLATIN
postmark 28 March 1923

Morristown, New Jersey

My dear Mr. Gallatin:—

Your letter was forwarded me here where I am taking a kind of "rest-cure."

You will receive this week the photograph. I have seen [Charles] Sheeler and he or Daniel will send it you. It is a very good photograph

Box 308, c/o Dr. Allen
Morristown, New Jersey

of the water-colour—I hope you like it as an example.

If you will send me a proof of the flower thing I should love to see it—I can return it at once if you wish.

Sincerely,
C. Demuth

TO ALFRED STIEGLITZ
16 April 1923

Box 308
Morristown, New Jersey

Dearest Stieglitz:—

I got your catalogue of your show several days ago, but could not make town,— missing your show and G'Kieffs—too bad.[1] But I saw Marin's! It was as "we" all know it was.

[1]A one-man exhibition of Stieglitz's (self-described) "life work" at the Anderson Galleries.

Mother said (out of the blue): "This—these are the only pictures which I have seen since the Ryder[1] show." It was such a strange remark from her. Of course, you don't know her. She is not easily impressed, and I did not think very responsive to "art," so called.

From varied sources come great enthusiasm, to me, of what you did of me and, too, Marcel [Duchamp]. Could you send me some of the old proofs, or any scraps, of mine so that I might see. I don't know when I will get to town.[2]

The serum seems to be,— well, it seems like a sort of trick. I feel I will wake; it is not possible. If it be true what it is doing,— then, well then, I can hardly imagine outside of our world,— too, there must be the few who "know."

Did you like the water-colour which I left at Of's? I thought that you might like to have it for a while.

Bobby Locher loved the tree things of yours. He says that they removed most painting, for him, and all photography! I don't think I've seen these,— I remember a tree in rain-drops or dew.

Love, dear Stieglitz,
Demuth

TO A. E. GALLATIN
20 April 1923

Box 308
Morristown, New Jersey

My dear Mr. Gallatin:—

Sent you your drawing the other day. Did you receive it. The "Met[ropolitan Museum of Art]" bought one of my things.[3]

[1]American Visionary Realist painter Albert Pinkham Ryder.

[2]Stieglitz had photographed both Demuth and Duchamp.

[3]*Flowers and Pine Cones,* 1918. Two months earlier, Charles Daniel had written to Ferdinand Howald that he was sending a Demuth flower painting and a pastel by Preston Dickinson to the Metropolitan Museum of Art at its request.

Your book, I [am] sure, helped. Thanks. Must one now I wonder feel "old mastery." I hope not.

With best and kindest regards,

Yours sincerely,
Demuth

TO ALFRED STIEGLITZ
21 April 1923

Box 308
Morristown, New Jersey

Dearest Stieglitz:—

Yes,— you are right,— all are blind. Well, we were told long ago that it is more difficult for a rich man to enter the "Kingdom" than for a camel, etc. As they grow richer they grow blinder.

However, I want to tell you—myself—having wired Mother & phoned Bobby [Locher] that the Met. did buy one of my old water-colours as you know, and, I confess, it means nothing to us unless it leads to more. Why mine should be there and others missing,— well, the gods alone can tell. But, as you say, it may lead to something. Of course, I don't want to seem to pose as not being pleased, but—for I am—but also a bit embarrassed; really; there are as you know one or two others. I will say one or two, but you "know" who should have gone into the "sacred" "Met" before myself, I feel,— that is, [to] be well represented. You know what I mean. They did take one of my best things,— which is lucky or whatever. All these things are so funny.

Dear Stieglitz, I would love to see you,— but I must grow fat. Already I've gained ten pounds,— so you see it may not be so long until I do see you.

Love,— yes, I send you both that—it is all we really have, after all.

Demuth

TO ALFRED STIEGLITZ
2 May 1923

Box 308
Morristown, New Jersey

Dear Stieglitz:—

You have me in a fix: shall I remain ill, retaining that look, die, considering that moment, the climax of my "looks," or live and change. I think the head is one of the most beautiful things that I have ever known in the world of art. A strange way to write of one's own portrait but,— well, I'm a perhaps frank person. I send it this morning to my mother.

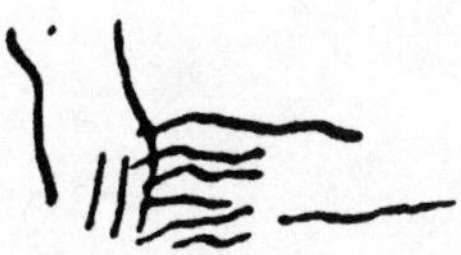

The hands, too,— Stieglitz, how do you do it? The texture in this one is— simply is![1] I hope that I see you soon. Thank you,— it seems so little to write just that,— but, as I say, I hope that I see you soon.

Thank O'Kief for the placing of the water-colour. The returns came in very handily,— all waters of life are expensive, be they waters for the emotions or for the flesh.

Yes,— I grow fat, 12 or 13 pounds. It is beyond belief, the power and subtlety of the serum.[2]

[1]In late April, Stieglitz made a series of photographs of Demuth's face and hands. Although the artist had gained some weight in preparation for this sitting, it is apparent that he was haunted by his illness.

[2]A month later Demuth was well enough to return to Lançaster "in marvellously improved condition," Charles Daniel wrote to Ferdinand Howald on June 22. "If it is permanent, and it seems so, truly a miracle. . . . 'Connoisseurs' who reassure quality by Dollars are beginning to notice him." Two weeks later, on July 7, he wrote to report a day trip to see the artist: "He lives in a quaint, charming old house, in a lovely 'American' city. . . . He is feeling quite well, and is planning his new work."

I will let you know what Mother writes of the photographs.

I heard of [Homer Dodge] Martin's sales. God,— what wonderful things the old man got. I really envy him. It was fine for Marin. I hope he got prices worth while.

Give my kindest regards to G'Kieff. I hope she is painting.

Love.

Sincerely,
Demuth

TO ALFRED STIEGLITZ
3 September 1923

[Box 308
Morristown, New Jersey]

Dearest Stieglitz:—

I was thinking about you for the whole day, Sunday two weeks ago,— and then your letter Monday morning,— even started to write you that Sunday—funny.

There is so little to write. Of course, you know the meager background we all have to work before, and with this fact, and the fact that I am completely cut off from any contact with ones interested in the "thing," makes writing hard. I don't know what will come of it; if I were a genius it might be all right, complete isolation,— and it is that here.

On the other hand I grow fat,— and fatter,— which is something! And I garden & cut grass and stay on the move,— as is expected, it seems.

There will be some water-colours for you to see in the autumn. Already there [are] ten or twelve which you could see,— and how I would like you to see them,— but you will. I've only painted in water-colour; the strain is greater, but I don't have to return and fuss if it goes bad as one always does in oil or tempera. You know I hate work really—that is, "art" work—I really do. I think that I only work,— but this will be too much,— we'll talk that out sometime!

Will you be returning in Oct? I'll get to New York at times. And maybe sometime for a month or two.

Best regards for G'Kief—and best wishes & love for you, Stieglitz.

Demuth

TO SCOFIELD THAYER
26 December 1923

My dear Thayer:—

The "Living Art" is with me.[1] It came last week. It is not difficult to write of it; you remember I was complaining about a "difficulty," when I saw you in New York.

My dear Thayer, it is beautifully done. I congratulate you on the doing. In my own case it is like getting my "tempera" back!—really. It hardly seems honest. I do hope it, "Living Art," meets the appreciation it deserves.

[1]In December 1923, *Dial* published *Living Art,* a portfolio of twenty paintings and ten photographs of sculptures by contemporary artists. Thayer contributed an editorial note. Five hundred copies were issued, printed in Germany by Ganymede Press. It included Demuth's *After Sir Christopher Wren,* 1920, reproduced in collotype.

In a few days I will be in town,— will call you.

With best wishes for the New Year and Living Art,—

I remain with you,
Demuth

TO A. E. GALLATIN

4 January 1924

My dear Gallatin:—

It is late to answer your letter, that, about your gift to the museum.[1] Please forgive me.

As you know I was very pleased, it will be remembered among the other charming things you have done for me.

I some times get to New York these days. I am "supposed" to be in improved health. I hope that I will see you on one of these visits, perhaps this month I will get to town for several days.

Have you seen "Living Art." The "Marin" is wonderful—the reproduction.

With best wishes for the New Year—

Yours sincerely,
Demuth

TO ALFRED STIEGLITZ

16 January 1924

Dearest Stieglitz:—

Your letter came last week. Thank you very much. I wish that I had some "go,"— such as yours. Mine seems to be used up these days after two or three hours of work and maybe a walk.

The exhibition chez D[aniel] closed after three sales—Cleveland one & Linshorn two, and one to Brooklyn—but I think of that one as a "gift" on my part to the museum!

[1] *Pink Cyclamen,* 1920, given to the Philadelphia Museum of Art.

Barnes is just back from France—"There has *[sic]* been important additions made to the collection." I wish that some "movie star" or whatever would make the art of the U.S. fashionable. Appreciation is too much to hope for,— but at times I think we may see it (our Art) become fashionable in our time. That would help, as you know, would be in one way "appreciation."

I am having a lot of fun—as much as I can have, at present, with the "posters." G'Keeffee's is well on the way,— Dove's and Marcel's are started.[1] I will send you G'Keeffee's when it is finished. The work on them seems endless. Am reading a book in which I find this advice: "for the lips of saints use Sienna & White; use Sienna first (for the mouths.)" "The Book of the Art of Cinino Cennini."[2] Also, "with prayers to the Virgin, and on a panel of chestnut wood coated with plaster & glue, paint the altar pieces."

Some time when you write me, send me Dove's address,— he and you sent me such a card, I want to thank them.

Your line of Demuths is out; after this sale? If you want, I will send you two or three small things which will be easy to get rid of if you move. There is at Daniel's some, and there is one there of the Bermuda ones which I would like you to have. If you want you can get it,— it is in a narrow gold frame. It hung on the left hand side as you faced the windows and hung on the wall at the

[1]This is the first extant reference to Demuth's "poster portraits," as they came to be called, although Robin Jaffee Frank, in *Charles Demuth: Poster Portraits, 1923–1929,* dates an unfinished study for one of Marsden Hartley a year ahead of the one of O'Keeffe. They are portraits of artists' and writers' work, sometimes but not always employing their names, either complete or in fragments, and featuring "objects and word play to allude to their life, art, and shared experiences," according to Frank. Her approach lends itself to symbolic and psycho-biographical readings that are not entirely persuasive. There is no evidence that Demuth ever executed a poster portrait of Marcel Duchamp.

[2]Cennino Cennini, *The Book of the Art of Cennino Cennini* (London: Allen and Unwin, 1922).

end where the windows are. It has a small piece of paper pasted on it,— over one of the roofs.

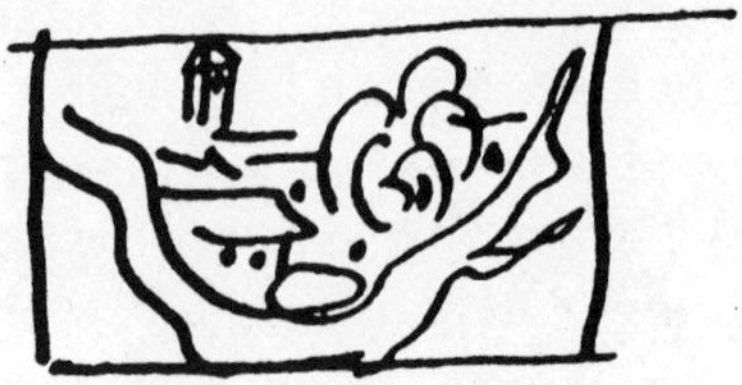

Demuth

P.S. Isn't the Down Town Marin in "Living Art" superb.

D—emuth

TO ALFRED STIEGLITZ
13 February 1924

Dearest S——:—

Write me the date of the opening of O'Keeffe's show. I will try to send, or bring you, the "poster." I'm still working on it, it may not come "off" at all. Dove's, I think, will come off.

About the Marin matter, I don't know. Would love to do it, but writing was always difficult for me. Now—oh my god!—everything is that. I'll try, some of it is already written, years ago, in my stronger period!

Love,
Demuth

P.S. She may not want to use it; there is that too. Even after the Hartley article.[1]

[1] Although Demuth aspired to be a writer, he published very little: a play, a poem, brief paragraphs about artists in exhibition brochures, an essay about his own work, a brief dialogue, and two impressionistic pieces; nor did he preserve many unpublished manuscripts among his papers.

TO ALFRED STIEGLITZ

postmark 15 February 1924

The Marin came yesterday,— will write.

The "poster" for G'Keeffe also finished itself yesterday in the general excitement of Valentine's day. It can be used,— three months; then suddenly it was done!

D.——

TO SCOFIELD THAYER

[circa February–March 1924]

Dear Scofield Thayer:

Pardon me,— but I've been really laid up.

But will be in New York this week. Will see you, I hope.

The storm—we will refer to it as such—is, I trust, past. The answer, in [the] last number of the "Dial," very funny.[1]

I've asked Miss McMillen[2]—the girl about whose wood-block prints I spoke to you—to send them. So if they arrive,— you'll know. Perhaps you will like them. The "cow" one I have. Best regards, Mr. Thayer. I forgive the slip about Charles.[3]

Yours,
Demuth

[1]In his monthly "Modern Art" column in the January issue of *Dial,* Henry McBride lauded American art over European art; he praised Thayer's *Living Art* and the fidelity of its reproductions in the February issue; in the March issue he inveighed against provincialism in both Paris and New York.

[2]Dolly McMillen, an acquaintance otherwise unidentified.

[3]Demuth invariably used his last name as a signature, and the last names of his correspondents in addressing them; he rarely included his first name; Henry McBride seems to be the only friend with whom he broke this convention in his letters, and he always referred to Marcel Duchamp by his first name.

TO SCOFIELD THAYER
[circa 28 April 1924]

Dear Thayer:—

I will miss it,— "the golden . . . ," whatever you called it. I remember that it was "golden" only.

Sorry. Some day we will go to Italy.

You may like Bermuda. It is very, very pretty there. Thayer, I was rather unhappy there, the winter of '17.[1] St. Georges is much the nicer. Don't be discouraged,— really it is pretty but quiet.

I will be in New York this week, and if all right will give the article [about?] Barnes into some careful hands at the "Dial." If this is all right, let me know.

I hope you find strength,— you seemed quite strong when I saw you. However, you must know.

Best wishes—Mr. Thayer,
Demuth

P.S. Did you receive the prints from Provincetown—

C. D.

[postcard of St. Peter's Church in Bermuda enclosed:] You see it's really pretty—I don't mean to be harsh—

TO ALFRED STIEGLITZ
2 June 1924

Dear Stieglitz:—

Thanks. Sorry not to have seen you before you went away,— wanted to bring you the Dove "poster" which is finished. It can

[1]In February 1917, Demuth had joined Marsden Hartley in Bermuda for several weeks, during which he executed his first works employing his unique version of Cubism.

wait now,— perhaps they will all be ready to bring you in the autumn. Already we write of the autumn!

Too bad that you are not feeling fit,— the country will, perhaps, rest you. It doesn't me. I hope that it will you! You too, I know, want a perfect thing,- you don't call it that, or do you? It does wear one,— still, it seems that it is the only thing worth wanting.

Barnes seems to be "out for" [Arthur B.] Carles at the moment. He resents his drinking, etc. & etc. He will soon be as moral as any well known preacher is supposed to be.

Tell G'Keeffe that I received the sample of board. It looks grand for working—haven't as yet been able to find out here what it is! Will take it back to New York when I go over.[1] I do want some for the two posters yet to come—Marcel [Duchamp]'s & [John] Marin's. I want all the help that materials can give for this effort.

Write me that you are feeling better,— soon. I'm about the same, am painting, & am on my feet. I know that this is enough really,— still I fuss.

Love,
Demuth

TO ALFRED STIEGLITZ
7 July 1924
Dear Stieglitz:—

How are you? I hope well.

It seemed about time to write. It seems that I always write you once during the summer,— if there is anything to write or not.

[1]By the end of the month, Demuth had been to New York for a few days. "He looks well," Charles Daniel wrote to Ferdinand Howald on June 30, "although that extreme care of living must be irksome. However, he had such a narrow escape that I daresay he is willing to endure much."

There seemed to be something when I started but now it's gone,— but I'll let you have it anyway. I know that you'll know that I was thinking of you and wrote, although there was nothing to say.

The photographs were grand in "Port of New York."[1] G'Keeffe's very grand. I had never seen it. Must read the book,— but don't want to until I've gotten all the "posters" out. I opened book at Dove, and it was surprising the way the essay & poster for Dove ran along side by side. It will be fun to see if they—the essays & my posters—all agree.

Let me know how you are. Love.

Yours,
Demuth

P.S. I'm working and about the same.

TO CARL VAN VECHTEN

19 August 1924

My dear Carl:

I'm sure we are the only two living "ones" who remember "that one"—Paul DeLongpre.[2]

Yours,
Demuth

[1]Paul Rosenfeld's *Port of New York* (New York: Harcourt Brace, 1924), a book about fourteen artists, had just been published.

[2]Nineteenth-century French painter who emigrated to California circa 1896, mentioned in Carl Van Vechten's 1922 novel *Peter Whiffle.* Charles Demuth is also included as attending one of Mabel Dodge's 1913 soirées at 23 Fifth Avenue, and he turns up as well in Van Vechten's 1923 novel *The Blind Bow-Boy.*

TO EDNA KENTON[1]

postmark [date indecipherable] 1924

My dear Edna:—

The titles?—there are four drawings;[2] I only remember two,—they are these sentences from the story. Near end Chapter VI this one: "She had picked up a small flat piece of wood, which happened to have in it a little hole that had evidently suggested to her the idea of sticking in another fragment that might figure as a mast and make the thing a boat." The other bit is near end Chapter III: "and I can see at this moment the way his hand, as he went, passed from one of the crenelations to the next." (You had this one.)

The other two drawings, one of which you had, the one of Miles & governess for final chapter, was, I think, but am not sure, called "Did I steal?" Now,— there—three accounted for. The other was of Miles & Flora in the garden with the governess and Mrs. Grose, and I think we could use this from Chapter XI: "They moved slowly, in unison, below us, over the lawn, the boy, as they went, reading aloud from a story-book and passing his arm round his sister to keep her quite in touch."

I do hope we can get the drawings, it would be fun to see us together in the arts.[3] Have written Mr. Parker & Mr. Daniel. He, Mr. Daniel, will see if the drawings can be reached—they have the titles written on them, I know, across the bottoms. Will call you when in town—or write me, Edna, if this is not clear.

Demuth

[1]American writer, historian, and leading member of the Heterodoxy, a group of professional women at the turn of the century, and Demuth's friend since the early days of the original Provincetown Players.

[2]Kenton had written an article about Henry James's *The Turn of the Screw* and wished to accompany it with four of Demuth's illustrations. It was published as "Henry James to the Ruminant Reader: The Turn of the Screw (with Four Drawings by Charles Demuth" in *The Arts* 6 (November 1924).

[3]Demuth refers to *The Arts,* the periodical in which Kenton's article was scheduled to appear.

TO MURIEL DRAPER[1]

25 January 1925

Muriel!!

Duck Fan, Law Bound,
Bags 'Em in Lunar Dark[2]

Demuth

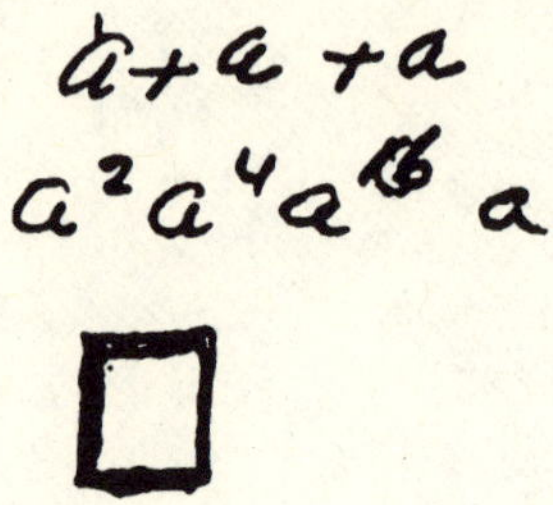

TO ALFRED STIEGLITZ

15 February 1925

Dearest Stieglitz:—

Ah, yes, that's what's been going on, illness—grippe,— ever since seeing you that day in New York. I was feeling a bit of it then,— but I thought it nothing "extra," but it was quite "extra."

The check came as you wrote about two weeks ago now, maybe longer. G'Keffe and I will go to see Mrs. W.[3] I couldn't write then, or would have written you.

There is nothing done, Duncan's is. And looks quite funny, to me. I will get it to you this week. Either I will bring it over towards the end of [the] week or send it to Of,— as it must be framed. If

[1]American interior decorator, writer, art patron, popularizer of the Harlem Renaissance, and social critic.

[2]This message is a newspaper clipping. Demuth's formula, following it, is inexplicable.

[3]Probably Alma Wertheim and her husband Maurice, the American financier and patron of the Theatre Guild, who were art collectors and member of the Stettheimer circle. Later Mrs. Wertheim married Paul Lester Weiner; she owned Demuth's *Peaches,* 1925.

I send it to Of will write you; perhaps you could explain about the framing if I don't make it clear to him, but I hope that I can bring it. Then if you want to show the three, Dove, G'Keffee, & Duncan, all right, and if you don't, all right.[1] I doubt if I do the others,— it's gone over too long a time for the heat to last, although I do think it, the heat, stretched for the Duncan one.

Oh, my dear Stieglitz, "Art is long,"—and a great deal longest, ain't it? The street, not Wall, would have been simpler, it seems, to-night.

Love,
Demuth

TO HENRY MCBRIDE
21 June 1925

It seems that you pick the cherries, my dear Henry,— and let them first, after the picking, stand (or hang) around for two or three days: not in the whole state but "mashed."

If the days and night are really warm about three days & night.

Then if all is well you press out the juice and to one gallon of cherry juice you add two quarts of water. Then you measure the amount and add two pounds of sugar to the gallon. Put it in a keg and let it ferment. Do keep the keg, or whatever, <u>full</u> so that the

[1]Stieglitz hung four poster portraits in his March 1925 *Seven Americans* exhibition at the Anderson Galleries to celebrate the twentieth anniversary of the opening of his first gallery, "291," although reviewers at the time were in disagreement over which of the poster portraits they had seen. The catalog accounts for six, including one of Marcel Duchamp, which Demuth never seems to have executed. In his 1927 monograph on Demuth, A. E. Gallatin mentions Marin's portrait as having been in the show. In his letter of 29 June 1926, requesting Demuth's additions and corrections to his monograph, Gallatin listed *Dove, Marin,* and *O'Keeffe* for 1924, which Demuth did not alter, but the artist added *Charles Duncan,* ostensibly for 1926, to Gallatin's list. Emily Farnham dates *Marin* to 1925; Robin Jaffee Frank dates *Marin* to 1926. The four—whichever they were—marked Stieglitz's first representation of Demuth's work.

stuff can "work." You must watch it,— for about two weeks, quite closely,— and keep it full, adding water, you know, as it ferments away.

This, my dear Mr. McBride, is all, it seems, that there is to it. I trust that you will be successful in your venture. If all this is not clear let me know and if you wish I will have my cousin (as you invented)[1] Ford[2] me down.

I really never make it myself but am around when it goes on.

My cousin thinks that you are grand. I am sorry we caused you that hour or was it only an half hour? Some time you must come up and see my real cousin,[3] here,— there is one.

How is your cousin,[4] better, I hope. I'll write you before my next visit, which I'm making soon.

Love,
Demuth

P.S. My next will be, I hope, less technical, more pure form, as W[est]. Chester has so kindly admired my English.

TO HENRY MCBRIDE

[undated, 1925?]

My dear Henry,

Are you still there? If you are and would like to see "my

[1]During the late 1920s, "cousin" was a popular euphemism among some homosexuals for a current lover or, alternately, for an intimate friend; whether McBride actually coined this usage cannot be ascertained. Also, it was used in the presence of strangers as a cover for homosexual relationships. Robert Locher employed it in a 1946 letter to Mrs. Rafael Navas in referring to his longtime companion, Richard Weyand; but in offering one of Demuth's erotic drawings for sale to Carl Van Vechten in 1956, Weyand wrote that he was a cousin—twice—of Locher's by marriage.

[2]That is, drive him in a Ford automobile.

[3]Christopher Demuth, son of Henry C. Demuth, Jr., who continued to operate the family tobacco shop in the house next door, following Charles Demuth's father's death.

[4]West Chester, Pennsylvania, resident Maria Pugh.

cousin" & myself, drop me a card, and we will come down, by Ford, to see you.

Yours,
Demuth

P.S. Didn't I look—in the Sep. "Dial"?[1]

TO ALFRED STIEGLITZ
[circa 5 July 1925]

Dearest Stieglitz:—

Was so glad to hear from you. Sorry about all the trouble,—but glad to hear it is passed, and hope now you will have a good summer. I expect to be here for the summer,— perhaps with a few weeks on Staten Island. The trees at Bobby's new house are wonderful—I thought I might do something about them.[2]

I want to finish the posters, too. Almost everyone has told me what a great mistake I made showing them without explaining that they were made for my own amusement! I'll do three, or more, more and show them all next winter. I'll make them look at them until they see that they are, so called, pictures. I wish I could afford to work without ever showing it. I think they don't deserve to see our work; most of them, anyway. I wish we could all "strike."[3]

Mr. Howald[4] bought two at the end of the season, and Mrs.

[1]Paul Morand devoted his monthly "Paris Letter" in the September issue of *Dial* to Proust's *À la recherche du temps perdu,* of which Demuth had not yet begun to read *Swann's Way,* the first installment.
[2]Robert and Beatrice Locher lived in a country house on Staten Island.
[3]Demuth's poster portraits in Stieglitz's *Seven Americans* show inspired frustration and resistance among the art critics who reviewed them—although Margaret Breuning, in the *New York Evening Post,* claimed they were "posters, placards, to notify the public, in symbol certainly, of something very true pertaining to each of the artists he portrays" (quoted in Frank, *Charles Demuth: Poster Portraits, 1923–1929*).
[4]Ferdinand Howald, who became one of Demuth's strongest supporters and collectors.

Force[1] almost took the large apple one which was in the show at the Anderson.[2] I couldn't come down, so it was off.

Tell O'Keffee to paint, I said, some more pictures as good as the two autumn leaves.

Love—to both,
Demuth

TO ALFRED STIEGLITZ
postmark 29 July 1925

Dear Stieglitz:—

Your nice long latest letter and then the "Dial"[3]—I once told you S[cofield] T[hayer] had a "pretty good heart"—and I once had to tell him that I would just as soon own a Marin as a M[ichel]Angelo! God, how we work. Still, on the whole, at the end of a none too brilliant winter, the photographs of "ours"[4] in "Dial" and T[hayer]'s comment was not so bad. What he said of Marin & G'Keeffe was really understandable and right—if anything is right,— all right.

I meant the two leaves, standing side by side, or on top of each other, red and gray—the colours were red and gray, the one you liked—it is a grand painting.

Love,
Demuth

[1]Juliana Force, director of the Whitney Museum of Art, then a former private residence in Greenwich Village on Eighth Street.

[2]Stieglitz's exhibition for the Anderson Galleries, *Seven Americans,* included paintings by Arthur Dove, Charles Demuth, Marsden Hartley, John Marin, and Georgia O'Keeffe and photographs by Paul Strand and himself.

[3]Henry McBride devoted his monthly "Modern Art" column in the July issue of *Dial* to a severe criticism of the members of the National Academy—"a set of fossils who cannot recognize art when they see it"—who were attempting to perpetuate academic painting and suppress contemporary art.

[4]That is, artists in the Stieglitz circle.

TO HENRY MCBRIDE

21 September 1925

Dear McBride:—

Cousin and I will be down, Wed. after-noon, if a nice day,—about four, if I don't hear from you not to come.

Yours,
C. Demuth

TO HENRY MCBRIDE

[undated, late September 1925?]

Dear Henry McBride:—

Your letter this morning. I don't think that Cousin & I can make, this week, our visit. I will write you again Sunday. It will be the early days of next. We go to Churchtown tomorrow; I think that will be all the Ford will do for this week.

Don't bother about the entertainment,— something can be arranged.

Yes,— no doubt that number of that magazine will be generally misunderstood. Frankly, I don't quite understand myself,—and if I don't,— well, what can be expected from the reading public. Rönnebeck—do you know him?—must still be having fits about it,— the poem.[1] I'm sorry S[cofield] T[hayer] is not to be in our country this winter. "Ah well, life is like that," as one of Mr. Firbank's creations constantly murmurs.[2]

So glad that you're still there,— and that Cousin & I will see you before the New York & winter season sets in.

Love,
Demuth

[1]The reference has not proven traceable.

[2]English novelist Ronald Firbank, whose fantasist novels Demuth knew through Robert Locher's frontispiece for one of them, *Prancing Nigger,* 1924.

TO GEORGIA O'KEEFFE
postmark 7 March 1926

Dear G'Keffee:—

Haven't seen you this season,— however, a few months of it remain. And I must be in town again for "our" flower show.

I did see your paintings. I looked at them carefully several times. I know that I never seem to look but I see pictures out of corners of my eyes. Your colour was the most exciting thing in this year's art world. Why it has not been more mentioned shows, for me, how stupid the art (painting) writers are; there it is looking like no colour has looked before and nothing said.

When we have our houses you must do my music room,— just allow that red and yellow "canna" one to spread until it fills the room. That would be grand. Perhaps it would not even, then, be necessary to ever have anyone play in this music room (unfortunately) of my mind.

There was a white "canna" one, not living, with pale blue and a little cutting yellow-green which I found as Hartley would say,— "Just right, Charles."

I hope you are able to get some into paying and understanding hands.

They are very fine.

Best wishes,
Demuth

TO ALFRED STIEGLITZ
27 March 1926

My dear Stieglitz:—

All right,— I'll too take the chance.

Will be in New York, if in this world, early Monday morning. I will send you the new poster,— will try to have you get it

Friday or Saturday,— it's framed and, to-day, dry. Daniel will bring you the water-colour which I want to put in the show and the other oil-painting,— about Friday,— no doubt, he'll not part with them until the last moment.[1] I'll bring the other few small things with me,— and be on hand Mon. morning.

I will send a few of the notices out from here,— if you send me about a dozen,— if you will, will you please send Howald one, from New York. I don't have his address. The notices looked and sounded very well.

Hope you like the "Marin" poster,— if you do, you & I will be the only two living things that do! I'm sure everyone will take it as an insult (not to Marin, however) I've put that on too thick, I think, for any mistake in that direction. I just went out to look at it, it's in the next room, and—anyway I like it.

Best wishes,
Demuth

TO AGNES BOULTON AND EUGENE O'NEILL

[circa spring 1926?]

Dear Eugene & Agnes:—

We couldn't get up, Mother & I, after the opera. I was sorry not to see you again,— I didn't see Eugene at all. Well,— you must come to see us in the province. Any time you are in New

[1]In April 1926, Stieglitz mounted his first Demuth exhibition at the Intimate Gallery. The "new poster" would seem be the " 'Marin' poster" referred to later in this letter (but see page 67, footnote 1). The oil painting would seem to be *Calla Lilies*. In the *New York Sun,* 10 April 1926, Henry McBride identified it as a portrait of an unnamed Bert Savoy. The painting was exhibited in a Stieglitz show at the Philadelphia Museum of Art in 1944 under the title *Calla Lilies and Shell*. In 1956, Robert Locher and Richard Weyand identified the figure as Bert Savoy, although this letter makes a clear distinction between a "poster" and a "painting." See Frank, *Charles Demuth: Poster Portraits, 1923–1929,* for a further investigation of McBride's identification. See also page 16, footnote 1.

York—and want to come over—or some holiday. It was nice to have seen you, Agnes; we did have a good time,— didn't we?

Bobby [Locher] writes that London may want him to do "Peer Gynt" or "The Sunken Bell" next autumn,— so we may all be there.[1]

I didn't see "Macbeth,"[2]— but he writes it was some,— and then some.

Did Williams send you copies of "Contact,"[3]— if he didn't I'll send you them through him. It's not much,— still, we must be in on our contemporaries.

New York seemed almost possible this time,— I suppose I see it for the first time,— but it was wonderful. I think it is changing. I wish that I could get drunk & see how it would look from my usual state of seeing it! No, there really seems to be some real interest around.

Let me know when you are coming down,— I'll come over.

Yours,
Demuth

TO FERDINAND HOWALD

postmark 13 April 1926

My dear Mr. Howald:—

Mr. Gallatin,— who will give you this,— is about to do a book about my work. He would like to see your pictures, those

[1] *Peer Gynt* by Henrik Ibsen; *The Sunken Bell* by Gerhart Hauptmann.

[2] Robert B. Mantell and Genevieve Hamper offered four of Shakespeare's plays in repertory that season.

[3] William Carlos Williams and the writer Robert McAlmon edited and published this little magazine; later it developed into Contact Editions, which published books by Williams, McAlmon, Gertrude Stein, Ernest Hemingway, and poet Mina Loy. Loy and and Demuth share a bed with Marcel Duchamp, artist Beatrice Wood, and actress-painter Aileen Dresser in Wood's watercolor, *Marcel's Bed,* painted to memorialize the aftermath of the scandalous Blindman's Ball in 1917.

of mine which you have and the others.[1] I, too, wanted to see them again this winter, but my visits are all more or less hurried or broken.

Mr. Gallatin has American pictures. You should agree.

Thanking you for this kindness, I remain—

Yours sincerely,
Charles Demuth

TO AGNES BOULTON AND EUGENE O'NEILL
11 May 1926

Dear Agnes & Eugene,

Don't you like my spring coloured paper—5 and 10[2] in any city of our country.

This is to remind you that Mother & I expect to see you in Lancaster, sometime before you go to the Cape. I don't know if I will make the Cape this summer,— I feel this spring that I've rounded all capes. Certainly I did that one,— once or twice when I was going.

Let me know when you get to New York, and, if all the signs are correct, do try and come up,— seeing me in my native surroundings.

Have seen no one in New York that you know, excepting

[1] *Charles Demuth,* by A. E. Gallatin, a handsomely produced quarto with a color frontispiece, an appreciative essay, and a generous selection of Demuth's work, representing his various styles, was published by William Edwin Rudge in 1927. Several letters subsequent to this one deal with its preparation. Demuth seems to have supplied Gallatin with a letter of introduction to Howland.

[2] A (now long outdated) reference to "dime stores," as Woolworth's and Ben Franklin's and similar businesses were called prior to World War II.

Adele.[1] Polly [Holladay] goes again to P[rovince]-town. There has been no word or sign from Eddy F[isk], poor boy.

Hope Bermuda was nice to you,— would like to see it again.

Love,
Demuth

TO ALFRED STIEGLITZ

12 May 1926

Dear Stieglitz:—

Would have written you, but expected to be in New York last Saturday,— couldn't make it. Will try and come over this Friday.

Thanks for the check. I hope you are still in town, as I do want to see you before you go away.

Have an idea,— to write about Florine S., Peggy Bacon, & G'Keffe,— "Our Lady Painters" or some such title.[2] I hope that it gets on paper. It would make the other ladies so mad.

Will see you Friday or Saturday. And if you are not in town will write you.

With love for you & G'Keffee,
Demuth

[1]American actress Adele Holladay (or Holliday), the protégée of the actor Otis Skinner, and mother of Polly and Louis. Adele seems sometimes to have passed herself off as her children's older sister. Despondent over the breakup of a love affair, her son Louis committed suicide in 1913 with a deliberate drug overdose—in the presence of journalist Dorothy Day and Demuth—at Romany Marie's, another Greenwich Village restaurant.

[2]Demuth tentatively titled this essay "Three" and wrote an introduction. He never completed it, although sections were later used as notes in brochures for O'Keeffe and Bacon exhibitions. Subsequently, it was published as *Three: Georgia O'Keeffe, Florine Stettheimer, Peggy Bacon,* by All Kinds Blintzes Press, in a limited edition, for a fundraiser at the Demuth Foundation, in 1998.

P.S. I wanted to see Miss E.[1] dance on Sunday. There was an interesting "Manet" of her in one of the papers. If you are putting in storage an[y] of your own collection and want to add the O'Keffee poster to them,— please do. I must have one "gone." They were so disliked,— could I afford it, I'd do nothing but!

D.

[From the Hotel de Crillon in Paris, Gallatin sent Demuth four pages with lists of paintings and questions. Demuth then returned Gallatin's letter, having added some interlineations. In this transcription, Gallatin's queries are printed in italics to distinguish them from Demuth's responses. Demuth's additions are underlined, except for his postscript.]

TO A. E. GALLATIN

postmark 29 June 1926

Hotel Brevoort, Fifth Avenue and 8th Street
New York, New York

I wish to list all of the illustrations and to note place of publication in the case of published drawings. My notes only cover the following:—

Zola's Nana. How many? 6(?)
H. James' The Turn of the Screw. 3?
" " Beast in the Jungle 3
Balzac. The Girl of the Golden Eyes. one
Poe. The Masque of the Red Death. one
and about 6 — for
Wedekind's "Erdgeist."

[1]At least one Demuth scholar has suggested the actress Elsie Janis for "Miss E." Eva Tanguay is just as good or better a possibility, because of Demuth's devotion to vaudeville shows. The drag queen entertainer Bert Savoy, whom Demuth admired extravagantly, was sometimes called ironically "Miss E" for Julian Eltinge, a refined transvestite singer. It is possible (but unlikely) that "Miss E." refers to Ettie Stettheimer, since she and her sisters were routinely addressed as "Miss" and since Miss Ettie did go dancing on occasion with a string of beaux.

None were published as illustrations.

Large painting of calla lilly in oil or tempera? [Demuth drew a line through "tempera."]

Represented in

Metropolitan Museum of Art

Fogg Museum of Harvard *correct?*

Brooklyn Museum

Cleveland Museum

Rochester Museum *others?*

Barnes Coll.

Phillips Gallery

F[erdinand] Howald Coll.

Lewisohn Coll.

Vaudeville drawings. about how many? What subjects besides acrobats and dancers? Drawn in Paris and at Lancaster [Demuth drew a line through "Drawn in Paris and."]

I have no idea the number—perhaps seventy-five or a hundred. Barnes has most of them; that I know. Perhaps you will be able to see them in the autumn.

Names of flowers you have drawn? tulips, zinnias, daisies, cyclamen native pink orchid

gladiolas.

What other "posters" besides these? Painted in 1924? & 26

John Marin

Georgia O'Keeffe

Arthur Dove

Charles Duncan

Following descriptions were written from memory. Are they correct?

Aucassin and Nicolette. Do these two stacks rear themselves against "a pale blue sky" (yes)

Two

Paquebot Paris. "her three, red funnels outlined against the sky"

P.S. Sorry, not to have been more prompt. Hope Europe is still proving enjoyable though wet. May come over the 21st of Aug.—for a very short visit.

Best wishes & regards
Demuth[1]

TO ALFRED STIEGLITZ
12 July 1926

Dear Stieglitz:—

Glad to get your letter,— but so sorry to hear that you were laid up. Hope the lake and summer will fix you up.

I've never felt so "low." There seems to be nothing, nothing. I haven't painted for weeks. Everything seems to have been painted. Have written on the three girl painters, but nothing very much,— outside the start: "Peace! the charm's wound up." Which lines I found in "Macbeth." And this one I wrote myself: "A good painting is not a floor covering, nor is it a complete text-book on some imagined esthetic principle."

I sent the water-colours to Philadelphia. The building in which they are to be shown is not as yet finished. And the paintings which are to show the French painters' efforts are still being collected by [Walter] Pach in Paris. No doubt, it will not all amount to much.

My lack of whatever it is, which has been going on for some months, has made me think seriously of a trip abroad. A very unwise idea for me,— still, I don't know that wise ideas have ever moved me. I'll go the 21st of August,— if I go. Bobby [Locher] will I hope go with me. Anyway it passes the time thinking about it.

Give my love to O'Keeffe.

[1]Demuth passed up two opportunities in this letter to identify *Calla Lilies* as a poster portrait of Bert Savoy. In Gallatin's book, a reproduction of it is titled *Calla Lilies: A Decoration.*

I saw Duncan this spring in New York and he seemed the maddest of us all. Oh, lord.

With love, dear Stieglitz,
Demuth

[To this letter Demuth appended tearsheets for pages 419–20 of the New Criterion with a review of "The Art of Being Ruled" by Wyndham Lewis, a book about an artist who "finds himself, if he is a man of intellect, unable to realise his art to his own satisfaction, and he may be driven to examining the elements in the situation—political, social, philosophical or religious—which frustrate his labour. In this uncomfortable pursuit he is accused of 'neglecting his art'. But it is likely that some of the strongest influences on the thought of the next generation may be those of the dispossessed artists." Demuth added the following note to the tearsheets.]

I think this was written by T. S. Eliot,— it gave me quite a thrill. I don't think the artist is ever "dispossessed"; still,— there seemed to be quite [a] thought. More than probably there is in Mr. W. Lewis's whole book.

TO AGNES BOULTON O'NEILL
[circa July 1926]

Dearest Agnes:—

Your, one can hardly say letter—one can hardly say note!—came this morning. And I hurry to answer it not because of its length but because I' ve been wanting to ask your husband something, and, as you didn't add [an] address to the early summer's letter, didn't know where to write,— just Maine seeming a bit general.

You know, maybe you don't, that I've painted several things which I called "Posters," for several American painters. I showed them last winter. Well, my dear, I've now done Eugene and as it has his name quite plainly on it,— I thought I would like to know if he cared if I showed it. It isn't finished and if he objects maybe I will not go on with it. Of course, he would see it before I showed it to the world. I only wanted to know, now, if he objects to the idea. The thing itself is very "up in the air" and outside his name will probably be thought by most to have nothing to do with Eugene. It was really, at one time, a thing I started as a poster for "The Moon of the Caribbees."[1] At least it will have that much connection. I can claim that if—if' the New York art public say that I just painted Eugene O'Neill across an old canvas and called it a "portrait."[2] I want to do one of Wallace Stephens[3] and then I think American "letters" will be finished. I did one for W. C. Williams.[4] Do write me, Agnes, will you? what Eugene thinks,— or let him if he wants.

No, I haven't read "Swann's Way,"[5] but it's been on my mind

[1]One of O'Neill's one-act plays, staged by the Provincetown Players in New York in 1918.

[2]On the basis of this letter, Agnes Boulton O'Neill assumed that Demuth's painting, *Longhi on Broadway,* which he executed three years later, was a portrait of Eugene O'Neill, although both she and Demuth had been out of touch with the playwright during the interim. O'Neill met the actress Carlotta Monterey in July 1926, for whom he deserted his wife and family. No further correspondence between Demuth and Agnes Boulton O'Neill has survived. The poster portrait he describes here never progressed beyond a rough sketch. Her error has inspired remarkable readings by art critics to justify the various images in the painting as they might apply to the playwright. See Frank, *Charles Demuth: Poster Portraits, 1923–1929.* Demuth only identified *Longhi on Broadway* in letters written at the time of its composition by its title and as a "still-life." The sketch for his proposed poster portrait of Eugene O'Neill and *Longhi on Broadway* bear no resemblance to each other.

[3]American poet Wallace Stevens, whom Demuth may have met through the Walter Arensberg circle and whose early poems in *Trend* and *Rogue* and first book, *Harmonium* (1923), he admired. Some scholars believe that Stevens's poem "The Public Square," published in *Harmonium,* was motivated by Demuth's Precisionist canvases.

[4]*I Saw the Figure Five in Gold,* based on Williams's poem "The Great Figure."

[5]The first volume of Marcel Proust's *Remembrance of Things Past* (À la recherche du temps perdu) had recently been published in translation in America.

to do so for some years, one or two. After your long letter about it, will get busy. It apparently put you completely out of business, and anything that can do that must be something.

Mother is well. You must come up to see her. I think she was very touched by Eugene. A very strange mother—that mother. In the autumn it is nice here. Maybe you can make it then, or for Thanksgiving, some fete day, when we can light the candles and call each other the bitches that we are.

Love, dear Agnes,
Demuth

TO GEORGE BIDDLE[1]
16 September 1926

My dear Biddle:—

I'll answer your letter, of to-day, at once, as I expect to go to New York tomorrow, Friday, or Sunday. Will call you up from town.

Some of my best water-colours are now in Philadelphia at the "Susqui."[2] If your brother[3] is interested in any one of those and will tell me which one after the close of that exhibition, if I am feeling rich & charming, I may be able to give him a, more or less, bargain! Or, if you can find one chez Daniel which you think all right and let me know which one it is, I might be able to arrange something. Of course if you ever want one for your own that can be arranged. I think painters should be kind to each other: mak-

[1]American Social Realist painter and collector, a long-time Philadelphia friend of Demuth's.

[2]The *Philadelphia Sesquicentennial Exhibition* at the Pennsylvania Academy of the Fine Arts. As a former student at the Academy, Demuth submitted annual entries for its exhibitions; often they were rejected and when accepted were usually hung in obscure corners, as more than one of his contemporaries noted.

[3]American financier, art patron, and collector Francis Biddle.

ing up a bit, in this way, for the general unkindness of the world toward them.

Perhaps I could come up to Croton for the day,— some day next week.[1] We can see when I 'phone. Would love to.

Yours sincerely,
Demuth

TO ETTIE STETTHEIMER[2]
[circa September 1926]

Dear E. Stettheimer:—

Have I ever written you before?— or is this the start of a probable "famous" correspondence? You may do the editing. Your letter was a surprise, a very nice one,— I, feeling at the time, forgotten by the world.

You write of heat and the Atlantic. I have only had heat, but a great deal of that and little else. The summer has not added to my work or to my charm.

Stieglitz wrote me after he had returned to Lake G[eorge] from, being in town, ill, and again about a month ago when he was able to go bathing and Georgia [O'Keeffe] was starting to paint after what you seemed to think was her first try at real creation. I suppose we must all give ourselves this thrill, now and again, no matter what form it takes with us.

[1]Croton-on-Hudson was a suburban bohemian center for Greenwich Village escapees. Mabel Dodge, Louise Bryant, John Reed, and novelist Floyd Dell, among many others, had lived there.

[2]American writer who published under the pseudonym Henrie Waste. With her sisters—Carrie, who managed the household and spent many years in furnishing an elaborate dollhouse, and Florine, who painted fantastic and intricate portraits of her family and friends—Ettie Stettheimer conducted an elegant and eccentric salon in New York's high bohemia during the 1920s. Demuth was a regular guest at their dinner parties and other soirees. Florine Stettheimer memorialized him in five paintings: symbolically in her portraits of Henry McBride (1922) and Alfred Stieglitz (1928); figurally in *Love Flight of a Pink Candy Heart* (1930), *Cathedrals of Fifth Avenue* (1931), and *Cathedrals of Art* (1942).

Did you like the story, "Happy Ghosts," in the "Dials" of July & August by Mr. Lawrence?[1]

Tell Miss Florine, your sister, that either the makers of funny post cards have lost the "art;" or I have lost my sense of the funny. I haven't seen one for a long time worthy to be addressed to her. I have worked some on the thing about her "Art in Painting,"[2] as Barnes would have it, and have one or two lines, among a lot of others, worthy of my subject. It takes longer to get words in their places than it does to get colours in to theirs. I have not painted this season.

Almost got abroad myself, but it fell flat,— the idea was to go this coming Saturday, the 21st. I think I'll make it up by insisting on New York for next winter. The provinces are overpowering.

Have had no word from Henry McB[ride]. No doubt, he is enjoying it,— seeing Gertrude S[tein] and etc., etc.

Give my love to your family,— as you come back to town the end of September? Will see you then, but send me the news, between.

Love, sincerely,
Demuth

TO A. E. GALLATIN
15 September 1926

My dear Gallatin:—

Will be in New York, maybe Friday—17th, or the early part of next week.

Are you expecting to see Barnes before you fix on the ones of mine for the book. He has one I would like to use as [a] fron-

[1] D. H. Lawrence, "Glad Ghosts."

[2] The projected article progressed sporadically over about four years, to be called "Three," about Georgia O'Keeffe, Florine Stettheimer, and American caricaturist Peggy Bacon.

tispiece, if it could be arranged without too much general argument. But we can talk this over when I'm in town which will be very soon. I'll 'phone you on reaching town.

Yours, sincerely,
Demuth

TO ALFRED STIEGLITZ
19 September 1926

Dearest Stieglitz:—

I'm going to New York to-morrow,— to start it all over again, you know, how "we" are apt to bloom in the autumn. And, also, you know spring finds us blasted, thus reversing the scheme of nature. I'm only going over for a few days, but hope to be there this winter. Gallatin wants to see me about the photographs for the book. And I suppose this will mean a visit to Barnes. I wish we could go around, on some of our visits, masked, as in 18th century Venice.

The water-colours in Phila. look very well.[1] They gave me a good place, in the light, for a change! I saw them last week. They also have a small room of Eakins,— those still owned by his wife,— they are quite grand. There is one of a girl singing which is a great American effort in paint. I understand she has raised their prices well into the tens of thousands, which I find an amusing idea, and will not come down.

My summer has been a very bad one. No painting,— and such a feeling of it all being too much for the ones really trying. It would be grand to have a bit of a background,— the effort to make that new each morning for the day is a great one, too great. Still, if we don't try, will there ever be one? At times the "church" seems the only answer,— but I don't "feel" religion, so called.

[1]The *Philadelphia Sesquicentennial Exhibition* at the Pennsylvania Academy of the Fine Arts.

The appreciation for the girls grows a bit,— but only a bit.[1] "She can use the last mad throb of red just as it turns to green, or the ultimate shriek of orange, calling to all the blues of heaven for relief or support," this I've written about O'Keeffe's colour,— written justly, I think—if none too well.

When do you return to town. I suppose the Lake is fine now.

I had a letter from Nice several days ago,— it said "Hartley has just finished some beautiful canvases, and is now packing up to leave for parts unknown to us." It added, "he hates us all and the south of France." How I can see it,— suffering Hartley.

Love,
Demuth

[Demuth enclosed a photograph of himself with a note on the reverse.]

This was taken four or five years ago, five or six weeks before I discovered I was ill. The scene is rather mad—isn't it?

TO A. E. GALLATIN
28 September 1926

My dear Gallatin:

I sent you the picture, Monday. I think the Hare one[2] better but this one which I sent may reproduce better. You can decide.

Yours sincerely,
Demuth

[1]"Three," Demuth's appreciation of O'Keeffe, Stettheimer, and Bacon.

[2]A watercolor of wild pink orchids, *Lady Slippers,* 1918, belonging to Mrs. Meredith Hare, one of Charles Daniel's customers.

TO A. E. GALLATIN
September 1926

My dear Gallatin:—

I could not find a photograph of the drawing of which we spoke—Barnes.

But I found one which I mailed you to-day. It was one of my good ones and I think the photo quite clear,— it was the drawing in the first Independent Exhibition.

I hear Brooklyn is to have a large Modern show, French & American—[1]

Best regards,
Demuth

TO ALFRED STIEGLITZ
12 October 1926

Dear Stieglitz:—

I must write you & tell you the news. I don't think it is, as yet, given to the public. The Susqui[centennial] Exhibition gave me a silver medal on my branch of plums, that water-colour you had last winter in my show.[2] It seems funnier to be noticed than not to be.

Love,
Demuth

[1]Société Anonyme, a forerunner of the Museum of Modern Art, was an organization founded in 1920 by Marcel Duchamp, Man Ray, and Katherine Dreier, in the belief—as Dreier wrote to Henry McBride—that "the modern movement . . . is a new vision in art" (quoted in Steven Watson, *Strange Bedfellows: The First American Avant-Garde* [New York: Abbeville, 1991]). By the time of the Brooklyn exhibition, the Société Anonyme had collected nearly two hundred pieces, many of which had been sold to Dreier by Walter Arensberg.

[2]*Plums,* 1925, now at Phillips Academy, Andover, Massachusetts.

TO ALFRED STIEGLITZ
14 November 1926

Dear Stieglitz:—

Am coming over Tuesday,— to see you and New York. Also Brooklyn & Beardsley,— Aubrey who with Oscar [Wilde] I still find to be great. And Marcel [Duchamp],— what a collection. I saw Marcel for a moment when he landed. What one's own time can do to one. The future makes it up, usually,— but dear Marcel, having used glass so often, seems to have added difficulties for the future,— of course, he would.

Of course, I want, too, to see the Marins. I didn't last year. I want Bullitt[1] to see them; he is the one who helped, if that were possible, Hartley. I think Bullitt brought some Hartleys over with him.

How are you? & G'Kieffe? Well, I hope.

I saw all the Stettheimers about a month ago. They seemed going strongly,— even Mother.[2]

Well, my dear Stieglitz,— Wednesday or Thursday then.

Yours,
Demuth

TO A. E. GALLATIN
22 November 1926

Montross Gallery
New York, New York

My dear Gallatin:—

Will you please give [Newman E.] Montross the water-colour which I sent you for your book, as soon as you can get it from wherever it is, or [when] they have finished with it.

[1]American diplomat and collector William Bullitt, husband of Louise Bryant Reed.

[2]Rosetta Stettheimer never recovered from her husband's defection and held her daughters—Carrie, Florine, and Ettie—in thrall with her periodic depression and semi-invalid state. (Two other children, Stella and Walter, escaped early on.) More than one friend believed that Mrs. Stettheimer's illness was self-induced and cultivated.

Will be back in town after Thanksgiving and will, I hope, see you & the new rooms.

Yours,
Demuth

TO ALFRED STIEGLITZ
26 December 1926

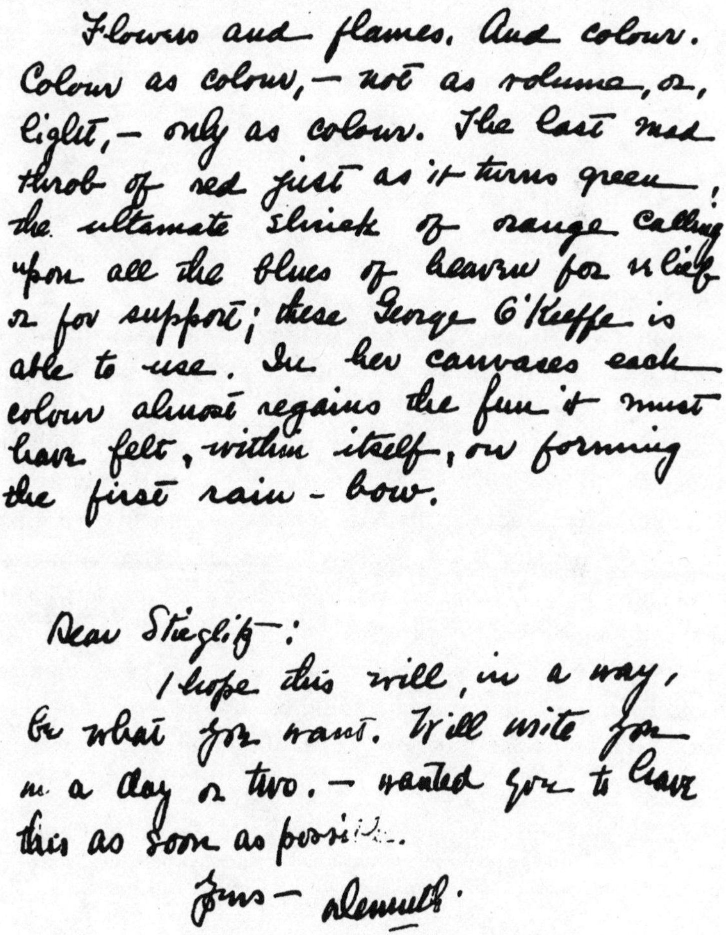

Flowers and flames. And colour. Colour as colour,—not as volume, or, light,—only as colour. The last mad throb of red just as it turns green; the ultimate shriek of orange calling upon all the blues of heaven for relief or for support; these Georgia O'Keeffe is able to use. In her canvases each colour almost regains the fun it must have felt, within itself, on forming the first rain-bow.

Dear Stieglitz:

I hope this will, in a way, be what you want. Will write you in a day or two.—wanted you to have this as soon as possible.

Yours— Demuth.

Flowers and flames. And colour. Colour as colour,— not as volume, or light,— only as colour. The last mad throb of red just as it turns green, the ultimate shriek of orange calling upon all the blues of heaven for relief or for support; these Georgia O'Keeffe is able to use. In her canvases each colour almost regains the fun it must have felt, within itself, on forming the first rain-bow.[1]

Dear Stieglitz:—

I hope this will, in a way, be what you want. Will write you in a day or two. Wanted you to have this as soon as possible.

Yours,
Demuth

TO ALFRED STIEGLITZ
2 January 1927

Dear Stieglitz:—

I want to wish you and G'Keeffe a very happy New Year,— and all the rest. The end of '26 seemed rather nice, perhaps our golden age is about to dawn.

Did Gallatin ever produce the water-colour. I gave it to him in October to have a colour-plate made for his book. I, when in New York, left a note at the Madison asking him to give it to Montross,— perhaps he did, but have never heard from Montross about receiving it. No one has seen it,— really everyone acts, even those supposed lovers of pictures, very oddly when they have them in their care. I had given Montross another, so I thought that would be enough, and that you could use the new one for Miss Carey.[2] It is really the only flower one, good one, loose. Surely a

[1]This paragraph was printed in the brochure for Georgia O'Keeffe's spring exhibition in 1927, lifted from Demuth's projected essay about O'Keeffe, Stettheimer, and Bacon.
[2]Possibly art critic Elisabeth Luther Carey; possibly just a Stieglitz customer.

colour plate can be made in three or four months! There will be some more flowers as soon as those come from Philadelphia. If this one Gallatin had has really reached Montross you could get it from him. Montross is all right about such matters,— better than Charles [Daniel].

The check is for the first payment (if it must be called anything) on the Marin. I can't take it,— much as I appreciate the "giving." I may never be able to give a real price for it,— but we can fix something about that too. The man on "The New Yorker" has been wonderful about Marin.[1]

The pictures which I have and my own, when I join the presumed blessed, will be offered to New York,— no one will get a chance then to buy any belonging to me—so that if I still have that particular Marin it will, if they accept, finally rest at 82nd St.[2] I put this all in this letter so that you will know and also that it is in ink.

Will be in New York sometime this month,— I want to work here for the rest of the winter,— not doing flowers.

Love,
Demuth

P.S. Glad you like the G'Keeffe paragraph. I'll do the longer one soon.

C.D.

[1]A parlor game listing the ten greatest American artists "never got beyond Marin, the one American to achieve immortality . . . , a steadfast poet, awaiting for his countrymen to catch up with him," *New Yorker,* 25 December 1926. In the following issue of the magazine, Duncan Phillips was reported to have purchased four Marins for $6,000 for his Washington, D.C., museum, so that "The Rotarian can now admit he likes Marin because he has become successful," *New Yorker,* 1 January 1927.

[2]At the Metropolitan Museum of Art.

TO HENRY ERNEST SCHNAKENBERG[1]

13 February 1927

Hotel Brevoort, Fifth Avenue at 8th Street
New York, New York

My dear Schnakenberg:—

Your letter was forwarded,— returning to its home town.

Of course, I would only send to the National Academy Exhibition if I were a member,— otherwise, who can tell? If the National Academy wish "some water-colours,"—they or it,—must first make me a "N[ational] A[cademician]."[2]

Hoping to see you before I go back to my province.

As ever, sincerely,
Demuth

TO ALFRED STIEGLITZ

21 February 1927

Dearest Stieglitz:—

[George] Of writes that he now has the water-colours from Phila. Will you get the two—the branch of plums and the other with the plums in it—from him. Maybe Miss Carey would like one of those. They, I think, will be 1000 each. Zola can get them some day.[3]

The Duchamp "movie" was very fine,— it gave me quite a

[1]Officer of the National Academy of Design.

[2]The National Academy of Design, founded in 1826, held annual exhibitions and later served as the foundation for the Metropolitan Museum of Art. Demuth's tongue is in his cheek in this letter: he would not have welcomed an invitation to join an organization so staid in its adherence to conservative tastes and traditions.

[3]The line is obscure; perhaps Demuth means that in time his illustrations for Zola's *Nana* will command similar prices.

thrill.[1] Dear Marcel,— and yet there are so many who think he is only so-so—or not even that.

Love— & for G'Keeffe too.
Demuth

TO HENRY ERNEST SCHNAKENBERG
[undated]

[telegram]
New York, New York

DEAR SCHNAKENBERG:—

I HAD PROMISED BOBBY L[OCHER]—TO SPEND THE DAY WITH HIM IN TOWN. FOOLING AROUND YESTERDAY I FORGOT ABOUT THIS—DO FORGIVE ME. I WILL SEE YOU AT THE GALLERY SOME TIME BEFORE GOING BACK TO LANCASTER. SORRY TO HAVE MIXED THINGS UP—

DEMUTH

TO A. E. GALLATIN
12 April 1927

Dear Mr. Gallatin:—

I was unable to reach Mr. Howald while in New York. His address is 1105 Park Ave.

I will send you a note, to him. It, I am sure, would be all right without.

Hoping your trip abroad proves what you wish.

Yours,
C. Demuth

[1] *Aenemic Cinema,* 1924.

TO GEORGE BIDDLE
16 May 1927

My dear Biddle:—

Your letter was here when I came back Saturday.

Of course you are to have a water-colour. I don't seem to care much about time anymore; sometimes it takes months for very simple acts. But I always meant you to have it,— so do take the one from Montross which you liked and let me have 200.

You can get it after that show which it is in has closed,— the closing date I've forgotten. I'll write him to give it to you. I told him when in New York that we might have an exchange or something between us. Don't say anything to him about price, etc. I think the show will probably close this week.

Will call you up,— when next in town. Must do some painting,— it's been going none too well now for some months.

Let me know if you take water-colour from Montross.

Yours,
Demuth

TO GEORGE BIDDLE
20 June 1927

My dear Biddle:—

Have received both checks,— thanks. No,— the price was 200. Can't do better than that.

The old Academy à Philadelphia[1] ha[s] asked me to be on jury for next water-colour,— November. Think that I will be able to get some nice water-colours in show.

Saw Adolphe[2] several weeks ago,— and Tyson's pictures,[3]— the pictures are few but all very grand ones.

[1]The Pennsylvania Academy of the Fine Arts, where Demuth had studied early in his career.
[2]Philadelphia socialite and Sunday painter Adolphe Borie.
[3]American artist, art patron, and collector Carroll Sargent Tyson.

Don't forget you and the Weed[1] are coming to see me, during summer. Am to spend part of July with Adolphe,— can't think of a madder place to spend July than your home town,— still, it's something I've never done. Who can tell?

Best wishes for a summer's work.

Demuth

TO HENRY MCBRIDE
27 June 1927

My dear Henry:—

You can get to us by Penna. R. R., or by trolley, which passes the door, from Coatesville or Downingtown.

Do come up Saturday. Frank[2] & I will return you to your hills and boxwood. Expected to write you earlier but I was in New York & our world has scattered for the summer and no one had your address. Mrs. Force was the last one whom I counted but she found that she had "those addresses" in town! I saw her Saturday in the country. Bobby [Locher] & Adolphe [Borie], myself, also Dr. Force, were lunched by her.

This morning I discover that I have mislaid it, too! "God"!— would say in such time, Mr. Hartley.

Let me know when you are arriving,— and I will meet you with flags, it being so near the Fourth.

The trollies (that word looks strange) from Coatesville pass the door every hour and I enclose a time-table of the P. R. R.

We, Mother and I, count on you my dear Henry. Maybe Bobby will be here with his sister [Lila Locher Roland].

Best regards,
Demuth

[1]American editorial cartoonist Clive Weed.

[2]Lancaster resident Frank Everts and his wife Elsie were intimate friends of Demuth; Elsie had been a student with Demuth at the Pennsylvania Academy of the Fine Arts.

TO ALFRED STIEGLITZ
29 June 1927

Dear Stieglitz:—

No,— working. Only my general lack of doing things when they should be done. The photograph came in good shape and is very fine. Your letter came last week just as I was leaving for a few days in N.Y. That is the reason that I did not answer it at once. Too, I really have been working,— quite hard for me these days. No one has seen these three new things,— I wonder about them from day to day as I work on them. Have a lot of things in mind but it is such slow "going" that I don't know if they will ever reach canvas or paper. McBride is to spend the Fourth with me, here,— I'll show them to Henry first.

I had a letter from Ettie [Stettheimer] to-day and she had one from Carrie [Stettheimer] several days ago. Carrie writes that several days after her arrival in Paris, Marcel [Duchamp] called with the news that two days before the call he had been married. A French girl and rather rich.[1] I hope that she is quite rich. He should be supported, if it comes to that, in splendor.

Your photograph of him is very telling. It hangs in my bed-room with the Marins & the G'Keeffes & a Currier & Ives called "Lydia Sower: a Morning's Walk." Lydia leans on a beehive, surrounded by sun-flowers, grasping a doll. The walk she has either had or is about to take, as I understand art,— which is about as near as any critic gets. Some that we know never get as near as this in a winter's work.

I think I'll be here the rest of the summer. Maybe go to the Stettheimers for a visit and to [Adolphe] Borie in Philadelphia. He has a nice place there, with a grand garden.

I think all my water-colours are still in New York. [Francis] Biddle bought one from me,— that is, no one got a commission. Although he hasn't paid me either! I think we are all fools, really.

[1]French automobile heiress Lydíe Sarazin-Lexassor.

Thanks for "Marcel."
My love to G'Keefe & to you.

Yours,
Demuth

TO ALFRED STIEGLITZ
[July?] 1927

My dear Stieglitz:—

Well, how are you & G'Keeffe? I'm still around and working some, so, I suppose, I can think of myself as all right.

McBride was here at the Fourth. He seemed to stand it,—haven't heard from him since, so maybe he didn't. He said that he enjoyed the Marin, in the morning, while he was still in bed.[1] I

[1]During his visit to Lancaster, McBride wrote to Florine Stettheimer: "It seems to be some day up here in Lancaster. . . . We have just had a hearty and delicious luncheon of turtle soup and champagne. It seems everybody, who is anybody at all in Lancaster, has turtle soup on the Fourth of July. It is a very 'filling' sustaining food and at the same time has a subtle flavor. . . . The Demuth house is a knock-out, as you might guess. It's in the heart of town, with a narrow entrance (decorated chastely by Bobbie Locher) that opens out into bigger rooms at the back, which in turn look out on delightful gardens, in which there is a long brick terrace and many brick walks. The flowers are plentiful and many of them are family relics that have nothing to do with the fashions of the day. The house is full of quaint furniture and some amusing works of art. Among the latter are things by Marin, Louis Bouché, Pascin, and Georgia O'Keeffe. There are no Florine Stettheimers, which I thought odd. One would look well in my room, which is all in white, with a wall paper of small dots at regular intervals. I told Charles he'd have to have you down here, but he smiled curiously and said he didn't think you'd come. And there's a marvelous church steeple to be seen from the garden—the finest I've seen in America. More or less baroque and foolish, but adorable. Square brick tower rises above the roof and the rest is in white wood, with four large prophets at the four corners. The tower contains great bells, which raise a frightful din on Sunday mornings at eight o'clock, but the congregational singing was charming from a distance of sixty feet. They wound up with 'America' so nicely, I almost wept." A few days later, on July 8, McBride sent a retrospective report of his visit to his friend Malcolm MacAdam. Several parties were given around town, including those hosted by Robert and Beatrice Locher, George and Francis [Biddle], and the last living descendant of William Penn. "They drink a good deal in Lancaster," he wrote, "but I refrained." McBride had a sufficiently good time to repeat the visit for the same holiday two years later.

sometimes look at it myself in the dawn, and think how someday they will be "appreciated,"— whatever that kind of "appreciation" means,— nothing really. Still, a few of us have lived, although it almost killed me—will in the end, I suppose—and are able through this living to see, before a thing is a safe old master, its living qualities.

Haven't had any news from the Stettheimers,— not since Ettie wrote me about Marcel's wedding.

You know that flower water-colour is still at Montross. If G'Keeffe really some time wants it, of course she can have it. I wish I could give them away to people who really like them & want them. It would make that part of art so much simpler. These terrible Daniels, etc., of our world.[1]

I would love to go somewhere—where I don't know—any place is almost impossible. Maybe it's just something that always goes along with me, that I'm tired of having around, and think a change of place would help me, there. I'm really all right here,— but at times I <u>almost</u> wish I could "go in for" hysterics; but all I can go in for is another picture. Well, there's almost four new ones of these to date. Henry saw them but showing one['s] own pictures to critics,— really I'd rather take them to the meadow and show them to a nice cow. It's more helpful!

I think, after all, I'll let you have this mad bit. I read over it and thought that I wouldn't, but I will. But don't ever print it.

I hope you are well,— as well as we can be,— we for whom every moment is either too wonderful or not wonderful enough.

Love,
Demuth

[1]Demuth's disenchantment with Daniel continued, despite this dealer's unswerving loyalty in supporting his work. Demuth aspired to be represented exclusively by Stieglitz. Earlier letters express his growing estrangement from his first professional supporter.

TO GEORGIA O'KEEFFE
6 August 1927

My dear G'Keeffe:—

That's the way for letters to act,— still, if we did write our best ones, they'd be so (at least mine would!) fierce, we could only keep them to read to ourselves.

I'm glad you got that water-colour; I hope you have by now. I wrote Montross & Of after hearing from Stieglitz. Have heard nothing from them but, no doubt, they between them got it packed and expressed to you. Let me know if you don't get it in a day or two. Sorry,— I couldn't give you that water-colour,— but, well, I'll buy one of yours some day. I should have loved to have the one of the sun taking a bite out of the sky-scraper [Alma and Maurice] Wertheim's one. That, too, is one of my troubles,— only wanting the best, so unlike the Metropolitan!

Have a flock of white butterflies—this is a canvas—started. I hope it turns out all right. It's much sillier than any of yours! There' s some white lilies in it too, not callas, Madonnas. It's almost Burne-Jones.[1]

Thanks,— best wishes to your work.

Demuth

TO GEORGE BIDDLE
10 August 1927

My dear Biddle:—

The party sounds grand,[2]— but I'm afraid it is no place for me! Now, that I know I can't be there.

Saw Adolphe last week and we arranged to come over together for it.

[1]English Pre-Raphaelite painter Edward Burne-Jones.
[2]Biddle had invited Demuth to a housewarming.

Then the Lochers whom I promised weeks ago to visit in Beverly [Massachusetts] say that this is the week,— so I go Wednesday to Boston.

Sorry,— but I know,— as they say,— "it is for the best." Have a grand time with the gin,— which, no doubt, you will.

Best wishes to you & Mme,— and the new house.

Sincerely,
Demuth

TO ALFRED STIEGLITZ
15 August 1927

Dearest Stieglitz:—

I am so sorry to hear about Georgia; I hope it was not serious, but with "us" everything is more serious than with the less sensitive.

I've been away for about ten days,— came back here end of last week. Was in Beverly, Mass., near Boston. I find, at the Boston Museum, that they have rehung and cleaned my favorite, of that time, painters' canvases, I mean Washington Allston. I think that I've spoken to you about his canvases, five or six, which they have. Now that they have been cleaned they are more amazing than ever. Using as he did the traditions of Stuart and, I suppose, West, he was able by some magic to produce these canvases which are if not in the class of the greatest "painting" only, a very little removed from it.[1] And, as I think of the portrait—one of himself—I'm not so sure it could not have [hung] with the greatest portraits and still be noticed. When I first looked at it, it seemed good, very traditional,— and then slowly it starts to "live"; slowly

[1]Washington Allston painted both portraits and classical landscapes and is generally regarded as the artistic descendant of portraitist Gilbert Stuart and landscape painter Benjamin West.

across its surface sweeps the entire "twists" which [Nathaniel] Hawthorne and [Henry] James tried to capture. Somehow it is able to say: "America doesn't really care,— still, if one is really an artist and at the same time an American, just this not caring, even, though it drives one mad, can be artistic material."

Glad you have the water-colour,— and like it. It was the last good one of flowers which I've been able to do. Since that one there have been no good flower ones.

Hoping G'Keeffe is getting along & will soon be able to be at work. With best wishes & love for you both.

Demuth.

TO HENRY MCBRIDE

19 August 1927

Dear Henry:—

Thanks for the so-called throw. Will use it certainly in a water-colour, hoping that its romantic history will give my water-colours a second youth.

I don't think that we will meet chez Florine; her mother is very ill again, so all, but Carrie, have returned from Europe, about 9 months ago. Of course, it will all be blamed on Florine & Ettie by Carrie, those poor girls.[1]

Alfred [Stieglitz] writes also from New York that he is there because Georgia is in the hospital,— for a time. Don't know any-more about it than this.

Robert & Beatrice [Locher] & Charles (myself) went to Beverly, Mass., since you have visited at Lancaster. We did Cape Ann completely, including the great points such as Harry Sleeper's[2] and

[1]Rosetta Stettheimer's real or feigned illnesses continued to influence her daughters' lives.
[2]Over a period of many years, American interior decorator Henry Davis Sleeper constructed "Beauport," an eccentric architectural collage of forty rooms, now a museum.

the smaller churches. In Boston, which I did alone, I found that the Museum had cleaned their Washington Allstons. They are grand. The [John Singer] Sargents on its walls are not grand, indeed they are not in any way grand. They also have all their Blakes hanging. They are grand. Have you ever seen the Boston Blakes.

Adolphe [Borie] was seen but not that night. He was visiting the Birch Bartletts in Beverly, a swell house—not our kind, but swell—with some good modern art.

Of course, you must return—if you liked it—for perhaps one of the quieter major fêtes. Cousin and I will probably call before the New York movement for the coming season sets in. Cousin wants to go over for the polo games, at least one of them, and I suppose that I'll go with him. Perhaps we will see David.[1]

How is your garden,— ours seems thin. Have painted no flowers, which means that I'll have less money next winter. How the collectors love flowers. Maybe the "throw" will start me again on my best known "line."

Well, Henry,— think that I've given you all the news that's fit, etc., etc., & etc. My best regards to your [*word?*] & to you yourself.

Yours,
Demuth

TO GEORGE BIDDLE
30 August 1927

Dear Biddle:—

Thank you for the check,— it will make the end of summer seem brighter.

[1]The reference has proven untraceable.

I hope to motor to Boston next week,— from Lancaster. And on the way will stop at Croton and see you,— with luck, that is. Will let you know next week for sure. We don't want to go into New York so may ask you to put us up,— or select an inn for the night,— for the two of us. Another man[1] (I hasten to add) & myself.

Haven't seen Adolphe,— or Philadelphia for some time. I suppose Borie has started west. He and Howe wish to look over my province some time after the end of September,— what for I don't know. Still, will be very glad to give them a Cook's tour of it.[2]

With best wishes & hoping to see you both next week.

Yours,
Demuth

TO ALFRED STIEGLITZ
30 October 1927

Dear Stieglitz:—

So glad to get your letter. You are probably now in New York. I was there when you wrote to me. Will see you in a week or two there.

Sent Daniel one of my new oils,— G'Keeffe can see it this week as I think he is opening up for the season this week. You can hear about it from her,— as you don't go around. Maybe there is nothing to hear,— I don't know; it looked none too brilliant when I finally sent it off.

Peggy Bacon did my portrait this summer,— I haven't seen it,— she did it from sketches—she's done eight or ten—in pastel. She said when I was posing that she was going to bring them in to you,— to see & also to see if you would like to show them. I

[1]Demuth's companion has not been identified.

[2]The reference is to the then most popular tourist bureau in America.

told her that you liked her drawings, and to surely show them to you. Alex[1] said some of those already finished were very good.

Saw Gallatin when in New York. I gave him a drawing; he seemed pleased. McBride & I had lunch with him.

Nice to hear that you & G'Keeffe got some work done by the lake,— do want to see it. Must say the summer didn't add much to my work. Tried some water-colours several weeks ago,— they were terrible. The field is to Marin,— if it always wasn't anyway.

Haven't seen the Stein book. But over the summer have read Proust,—[2] so I've joined the others,— not without reservations, however. It's too much like myself for me to be able to get a great thrill out if it all. Marvelous, but eight volumes about one personal head-ache is almost unreadable, especially when you have your own head-ache most of the time.

Best wishes for the coming season—& love to you & G'Keeffe.

Yours,
Demuth

TO ALFRED STIEGLITZ
20 November 1927

Dear Stieglitz:—

Have written to Montross to give you all the things of mine which he has, so after you receive this you can get them. I wrote him at the same time as this.

If the oil is finished soon will send it to you, or bring it when I come over.

[1]American Neo-Realist painter Alexander Brook, Bacon's husband.

[2]Gertrude Stein's thousand-page novel *The Making of Americans,* published in France in 1925 and in America in 1926, about which there was publicity and notoriety; Stein published no books in 1927, but the first four volumes of Marcel Proust's *À la recherche du temps perdu* had been translated and published in America by that time. It was longer even than *The Making of Americans,* which motivated Demuth's linking the two writers here.

Things are upset here but maybe I'll get some work done,—there's really little to do on that one anyway.

Best wishes to you & the Marins.

Demuth

TO A. E. GALLATIN

4 January 1928

Dear Gallatin:—

That drawing, illustration, was one for the "Nana" set which was not used because that scene was really in another Zola novel, the name of which I, at the moment, have forgotten.[1] The child is Nana herself as they say, now, in the "movies." I think that drawing was once entitled "Le debut."

About the lunch, I will come if I possibly can. Things have been very upset here for me for the past month. I think I can arrange to come to New York Saturday. Will call you Saturday around six if in town,— if I don't call you will know that I could not make it.

Best New Year's wishes.

Yours sincerely,
Demuth

TO ALFRED STIEGLITZ

13 March 1928

Dear Stieglitz:—

Here is what I did for Peggy Bacon.[2] If you don't like it destroy it. I write with more pains from year to year. I worked

[1]The scene was from Zola's *L'Assommoir.*

[2]Part of Demuth's projected essay, "Three." Stieglitz used the section on Peggy Bacon as a catalog note, titled "A Foreword," for her exhibition in 1929 at the Intimate Gallery.

hours on this,— strange as it may seem. The opening lines are by Poe.[1] I think it got a bit sharp.

Demuth

TO ALFRED STIEGLITZ

4 June 1928

Dear Stieglitz:—

It's almost time for you to be going, I suppose. I wish that I could too, go to the sea, some place on the Mad Cape,— Cape Cod. This morning I got from there a lot of wild pink orchids,— I painted them once—Mrs. Hare has it—my really best flower piece.[2] I wanted it used for the first water-colour of my book,— of course it wasn't.

I'll stay here & work,— I don't see anything else. I like a few places and a few people but I see them seldom. Perhaps I wouldn't work at all if I did,— still, I don't like most of my work, and maybe that's what keeps me working.

Will you see that the "Plums" water-colour gets to Of? I'll write to him to send it on to me. And I forgot to ask you that day if you found a photograph which would do for [Frank] Crowninshield? Anyway, he's now in Europe, if you didn't. He can have it in the autumn.

If you happen to see a book called "Armed With Madness," by Mary Butts, look it over. There is something quite terrible of

[1]Edgar Allan Poe: "Yet we have heard discoursing of carpets, with the air *d'un mouton qui réve,* fellows who should not and could not be entrusted with the management of their own moustaches. Every one knows that a large floor may have a covering of large figures, and that a small one must have a covering of small—yet this is not all the knowledge in the world." This passage has not been identified. At the beginning of his introduction to the manuscript, Demuth quoted Shakespeare: "And thrice again to make up nine, / Peace! The chain's wound up" (*Macbeth* I:3,36–37).

[2]*Lady Slippers,* 1918, now in the permanent collection of the Munson-Williams-Proctor Museum of Art, Utica, New York.

our times about it. I've just finished it,— maybe that's what['s] the matter with me.

Of did me a beautiful frame for my yellow flowers,— I can use it on some others, expensive but still. It's what I wanted for the now famous "peaches." And only g[o]t three years after. Still, now that I know he knows what I want and can do it,— well, I can get it again,— maybe!

Will send you some money,— for the Marin, soon. Hope the Lake is as always, still, lakes don't change much. Hope, also, Georgia is alright, and that you will get what you want out of the summer. Tell her I hope she paints some "sweet" pictures.

Love.

As always,
Demuth

TO ALFRED STIEGLITZ
18 June 1928

Dear Stieglitz:—

So sorry to hear about all that attended your getting away from New York. And hope that by this time it is all straightening itself out.

The water-colour, the "Plums" (not Peaches this time) came in good time & condition. So Marin likes this one,— that will send its price up. He after all should know. Well, I've talked Marin for,— can it now be twenty-five years? anyway, some years before I ever saw him and long before I knew you which was in 1913, and some years before water-colour came into my own life. Funny,— last week I was in the Academy in Phila. The rooms were empty, they were re-hanging the pictures, and I sat for a while in the large room thinking of my past. After some time,— well, I thought, right there at the end is where I saw the first Marins,— one was a flower thing. I remember it as being rather grand,— have never seen it again. When I looked again at the wall there was a grand flower piece. The men had hung a canvas by Twachtman, a good one.[1] I never knew they had it. It is very fine. I left,— for a moment I had the feeling that I could have made those men bring any picture into the room and hang it,— any that I remember and again wanted to see. Funny!

I haven't seen "Creative Art," but Lee[2] wrote asking me to write about myself for an autumn number. I don't think that I can, I'm sure of it. Maybe I'll offer him the thing about Florine, G'Keeffe, and Peggy Bacon. It may be finished by autumn.

Tell G'Keeffe that I got the piece of board which she sent me. I thought the box in which it was contained a frame from Of and had it sometime before I opened it. On opening found board,— it looks very helpful as to surface. I need help where I paint with oil-colour. Thank her for it for me. I haven't painted for some month[s],— I feel all in, or all out. I expect I'll start some day soon,— the flowers are all around the garden,— I can only look at them and dig around them so far this season.

Love,
Demuth

TO ALFRED STIEGLITZ
6 August 1928

Dear Stieglitz:—

I wonder how you are? Are you well,— or as near well as we, any of us, ever are, or maybe need to be. I hope that you are, however, quite all right again.

[1]American Tonalist painter John Twachtman, whom Demuth earlier associated with Georgia O'Keeffe as the only other "colourist" in American art.

[2]Lee Simonson, American scenic designer for the Theatre Guild and editor of the fine arts and letters journal *Creative Art,* a friend of Demuth's since the winter of 1912–1913, when they met in Paris.

Thanks for sending me "Creative Art." The Hartley, no, I don't know,— anyway the paintings—his paintings—looked very well. Has he gone back? Europe was to us all nearer & dearer, but,— well, you know. What could any of us add to Europe? Perhaps I like to suffer. At times I think I do. It may never flower,— this our state, but if it does I should like to feel from some star, or whatever, that my living added a bit,— for in this flower, if it does, I can imagine Rome in its glory looking very mild.

Which I suppose all brings me back to my work which has been going, but going very strangely this summer. They—the paintings—have a strange, inner strange look about them. They look sometimes like I think my own things do or should and then again when I look at them they seem to look very different & strange with a strange strangeness. Really, I can't tell,— you'll see them unless they look too strange some morning and I do away with them,— only remembering the summer of '28 without any work to help me remember some terrible days.

Am sending you some money. Kraushaar [Gallery] did all in all very well,— first year and his fear of high prices for water colours. Next year I'll surprise him with prices,— and not only him, I hope.

I think this, after reading it over,— so far, is pretty bad or maybe pretty good. I think my critical sense is failing too,— still, I let you have it. Perhaps what it's all about could not be gotten into words anyway! However, some one quite recently told me that my much discussed "Peggy Bacon" had two or three sentences of purest English.

Give my love to G'Keeffe and love for you.

Yours,
Demuth

TO ALFRED STIEGLITZ
6 November 1928

Dear Stieglitz:—

I wonder how & where you are. Florine [Stettheimer] seems to think that you are still in Lake George. I'm sending this letter there. I heard from Florine several days ago. Until then I hoped that you were back in town and to see you from week to week. I may go to New York on Friday, and may see you after all, as I want to stay a week or two.

I received your letter and check which I've put in the bank, but, really, I must talk this over with you when I see you. I don't see why the money isn't yours.

My work has gone very badly this past season,— I feel that I'll never get ahold of it again. My living and my work seem, at the moment, quite beyond control, both smothered by trifles. Of course, I know this happens to one, at times, but this time it seems involved past straightening out.

Have you heard anything about [D. H.] Lawrence's new book: "Lady Chatterly's Lover"? Do read it, if you can get ahold of a copy. I think it is a very great book. There is hardly anything that couldn't be said against it,— and yet,— and yet!

I was so hoping to see you,— I can't write in my present state. But maybe I will see you, maybe you'll be back.

Give my love to Georgia,— I hope she is working & well enough to work. I hope, too, that you are better and ready for the new season.

Yours, with love,
Demuth

TO ALFRED STIEGLITZ
[12?] December 1928

Dear Stieglitz:—

The Marin came Saturday,— I was away. I was home Sunday so I opened it,— it looks wonderful and with the others forms quite a provincial collection,— however, the province won't get them; not this one, anyway. I'll send you some money in a week or two.

I was in Phila. Saturday to see the new gallery open.[1] It looks quite well,— and she[2] collected ten or twelve Marins,— maybe not quite that many; I loaned mine of last year,— the tooth-pick one.[3] There is a very fine early one,— one of Sam White's.[4] Quite early, I don't remember having seen it before.

I expected to come to New York yesterday, but something happened so now I don't think that I'll get over before the holidays.

My red & gold picture is about finished and I'll send you that in two or three weeks—as soon as it's fit to travel.[5] It looks almost American. I hope that it will to you. Maybe I'm only fond of it as one is of a new shirt.

With this I'm sending you what I've written for Lee Simonson. Do let me know if you consider it "too light." Send it back to me,— I may add some bits here and there, but it will be like this if I do it at all. He got Gallatin to write me last week asking if I would not write one of the articles. I've written him that I would and that he should give me Feb. or March,— he never

[1]Probably the Little Gallery of Contemporary Art.

[2]The reference has proven untraceable.

[3]*Boat Off Deer Isle, Maine, No. 4,* 1926, with a border of bold hatchings.

[4]An early Demuth collector, Samuel S. White III and his wife Vera later established a collection in their name at the Philadelphia Museum of Art.

[5]*I Saw the Figure Five in Gold,* 1928–1929, Demuth's poster portrait of William Carlos Williams.

answered, maybe the letters went astray. If you see him and think that what I'm sending you could be used after a month or two of work on it tell him I'm doing it. What I'm sending you will be its general idea if it can be called an idea. Tell Lee it will be under a thousand words,— he wanted 1500. I couldn't write a 1500 word thing on this subject [in] under fifty years.[1]

How are you? I hope standing New York. I'm about the same,— if I were a woman I would know what was the trouble with me,— at my age. But as it's been proved that I'm not, well, maybe I'm only in need of a change of scene. Most of the time I'm far from bright.

Hoping you and Georgia are all right.

With love for you both,
Demuth

TO ALFRED STIEGLITZ
3 January 1929

Dear Stieglitz:—

Happy New Year to you & Georgia.

Many thanks for the letter about what I wrote for Lee [Simonson][2] & for the "Sex locked out" by D.H. L[awrence]. I think he really enjoys things for what they are and doesn't find it necessary to call them, after he has enjoyed them, by some other name. I wish our country could act the same.

I'll be in New York next week, I hope. Tried to come this week but have, I'm afraid, started a cold. I want to get some pho-

[1]"Across a Greco Is Written," a brief essay in which Demuth attempted to explain his work and set it in the context of the history of art. See the introduction to this volume.
[2]See footnote 1.

tographs of some of my things around New York. I've never had very many,— just a few and those not of the ones I liked best. I would like Lee to use the still-life which I brought to New York last year,— the one you have with the masks.[1] I wrote him to see you about it. I'll try and attend to the others next week.

The new oil you will have next week too.[2] I looked at it today and it seems dry enough to travel. I can varnish it there sometime,— take it to Florine's if you really want to show them later. I wonder what you will think of the new oil.

Am anxious to see the Hartleys,— haven't seen any since those four or five years ago,— in the big mixed show which you had up-stairs. You will find a check,— for past payment on new Marin. It is very grand, I think.

Must start some new things,— would love to do something of Broadway,— maybe I can do something of it here. Will try to see a lot of it when in town. Of course, you really never do see a thing when you look at it. I think that it's when the thing looks at you that you see it. And that can't happen in my now so short visits to New York. However, I may have luck—I've thought of it for some years.

Hoping to see you next week.

Yours,
Demuth

[1]*Longhi on Broadway,* which has often been misidentified as a poster portrait of Eugene O'Neill. In several letters, Demuth refers to this painting, never mentioning any connection with O'Neill. He calls it an "oil" and a "still-life" and then finally titles it.

[2]*I Saw the Figure Five in Gold.*

TO ALFRED STIEGLITZ

9 January 1929

Dear Stieglitz:—

I sent you my new painting to-day.[1] I hope to see you Sat.

Yours,
Demuth

TO ALFRED STIEGLITZ

16 January 1929

Dear Stieglitz:—

To-day I sent you my newest oil painting,—[2] I sent it collect and will fix that with you when I see you. I'm coming over Thurs. or Friday. I want the painting to have a glass but I wanted you to see it before. I'll take it to Of the end of week. It must, too, have some other frame. This was the one I wanted Mrs. Wertheim to have with her G'Keeffe,— but she hardly speaks to me now, so I suppose she will never own it. I hope you like the picture,— so few will,— l think it is quite funny.

How is G'Keeffe,— better I hope,— and too, I hope her show is going. It looked so well that Sunday.

Will see you soon.

Love,
Demuth

[1] *I Saw the Figure Five in Gold.*

[2] See footnote 1.

TO ALFRED STIEGLITZ
5 February 1929

Dear Stieglitz:—

The check came, Friday I think it was—thanks. I saw Mrs. Wertheim at Gene's "opening,"[1] and she was very nice! Pinched or patted my arm, in passing. Yes,— really, people who buy pictures are queerer than those who do not.

And Eugene's opening,— well, it certainly was a surprise. You got through it, and were interested almost all of the time. Florie [Stettheimer] & I decided—of course, we are not easily pleased—that he has used all the "tricks" beautifully, but so far as having any real quality (or whatever you call it), it hasn't!—any at all. But you must see it. It's one of those things,— but really not much more.

Does the picture, now that it's under glass, look all right? If it doesn't look "perfect," when I'm again in town will have it taken out and work on it again. I never expect it really to be complete,— that one is one of that kind.[2]

So Marsden is again with us. What joy & sorrow—just like Life itself. Tell him not to return until I have seen him. Lee Simonson wishes him to call him up,— he's in the 'phone book—12th St.—I think he said. Also said that he had a good cook,— that will interest M. Have you seen Hartley's pictures,— how are they? Those old ones—Daniel had some in recent show—looked very grand. Did I speak to you about them,— intended to, but don't remember doing so.

Let Florine see my new painting if it looks alright,— I told her you would show it to her,— maybe she isn't interested. Have been working on the others. They'll be finished by spring! They will not be so good,— I think the "still-life" my best picture so far.

The news of Marcel is strange. Still, he is stranger than any of

[1]*Dynamo* by Eugene O'Neill opened 11 February 1929.
[2]*Longhi on Broadway* is a still-life, unique among Demuth's oils.

us,— and that's writing a lot! But a great painter. The big glass thing, I think, is still the great picture of our time.[1]

Love—best wishes for G'Keeffe
Demuth

TO GEORGE BIDDLE
14 March 1929

Hotel Brevoort, Fifth Avenue at 8th Street
New York City

Dear George:—

Florine Stettheimer would like you to come with me to a party which she is giving Saturday evening,— an after dinner party. Let me know, here,— or call her: Circle 1428.

Yours,
Demuth

TO ALFRED STIEGLITZ
24 March 1929

Dear Stieglitz:—

Here is the Williams verse ["The Great Figure"]—the other one I want to call "Longhi on Broadway."[2] I haven't said anything to Kraushaar,— so, if you show them,[3] I'll write him, or you can tell him.

Love,
Demuth

[1] *The Bride Stripped Bare by Her Bachelors, Even,* 1915–1923, Duchamp's monumental construction of metal, wire, oil, and glass.

[2] Pietro Longhi was a late Italian Renaissance artist noted for his canvases depicting high-life among the intelligentsia of his time.

[3] Stieglitz's Exhibition XIX of five Demuth paintings—listed as *I Saw the Figure Five in Gold; Longhi on Broadway; Design for a Broadway Poster; Red Cabbages, Rhubarb, and Oranges;* and an unidentified 1918 *Provincetown*—in May 1929, was the last show held at his Intimate Gallery before he opened American Place.

TO ALFRED STIEGLITZ

1 April 1929

Dear Stieglitz:—

I don't care when you show the paintings,— it will be rather fun, as they are so few, having them end the so called season for art.

About the water-colour, do you think 1400 would be too high? I know, from the quiet of the country, that I won't do many like that one, no matter how long a time I paint. Whatever you think, also, it being Goodwin.[1] It's been so long a time since I painted a water-colour just that good,— maybe I never did, in some ways,— that I don't much care, unless I get a good price if I sell it, or not. I'd like to give it away—if I were really rich—to Georgia, or Robert [Locher], or Muriel [Draper], all having seemed enthusiastic about it. Oh, dear, I'm so tired,— I think only the grand manner would rest me.

You can price it as you feel about it,— it will be all right.

Yours,
Demuth

TO EDWARD FISK

6 April 1929

Dear Eddy:—

At some time after Xmas I got your prints, thanks,— they were a great surprise,— and I liked them very much.

Have been wanting to write you for a long time, and started to once from New York. It seemed as though it would be more to the point writing you from New York than from here. Here, being the end of our world.

[1]Art collector Philip Goodwin bought *Red Cabbages, Rhubarb, and Oranges,* 1929. Later, he traded this painting through Stieglitz for *Green Pears,* 1929.

New York has gone quite mad. It seemed once that only we were that way—now, everyone has taken it up.

How many years is it, since I've seen you? It seems rather many. I don't quite remember, where were we? Anyway it was before "Strange Interlude,"[1] which after all, wasn't so strange. And the latest, "Dynamo." Well, my dear,— ask me, ask me, about that one. My god,— he is now in Paris,— Agnes is in Reno. Well, Paris on a rainy evening and Eugene,— or, rather Eugene & a rainy Paris evening,— what a good time he can show his gloom,— but what comes out of it? I like fun to come out of our sufferings. I'm growing old. I only like the light,— unless it's really heavy.

Have you read the Proust which has been, so far, translated? That's what I call suffering. I suppose that you have but,— well, I must talk this over with you some time. I can't write about Proust. He wrote about it himself. I couldn't add anything.[2]

Was in New York not so long ago,— before Easter. Saw Peggy Johns, Rhy,[3] Polly [Holladay]. Haven't seen any of them in years.

[1]Eugene O'Neill's five-hour, nine-act play *Strange Interlude,* in which the character "Charles Marsden" is based, unflatteringly, on Demuth and his attachment to his mother. O'Neill's long-winded description is carefully veiled and even deliberately altered but clear to anybody who knew Demuth: "He is a tall thin man of thirty-five, meticulously well-dressed in tweeds of distinctly English tailoring, his appearance that of an Anglicized New England gentleman. His face is too long for its width, his nose is high and narrow, his forehead broad, his mild blue eyes those of a dreamy self-analyst, his thin lips ironical and bit sad. There is an indefinable feminine quality about him, but it is nothing apparent in either appearance or act. His manner is cool and poised. He speaks with a careful ease as one who listens to his own conversation. He has long fragile hands, and the stoop to his shoulders of a man weak muscularly, who has never liked athletics and has always been regarded as of delicate constitution. The main point about his personality is a quaint charm, a quality of appealing, inquisitive friendliness, always willing to listen, eager to sympathize, to like and to be liked." Marsden Hartley's name, rather than his personality, was employed.

[2]By 1929 six of the eight volumes of *À la recherche du temps perdu* had appeared in English translation.

[3]Peggy Baird Johns and her husband, poet Orrick Johns—nicknamed Rhy—who was part of the Imagist group of writers associated with *The Glebe*.

Rhy looked as he did when I first saw him, maybe a little older. He asked if I had heard anything from you.

Haven't seen any new painters, myself, in New York—but I'm told that some of the new men are wonderful,— well,— after all one can only tell from their paintings,— unless it's love,— and their paintings that I've seen have just been paintings—you know, nice, serious pictures. They're not as good as we were—and, I'm sure, not so full of fun, judging from the way they paint. However I may be wrong, must look over the field carefully some time, when I've time.

Let me know if you come up north—maybe, you'd like to come here & see me for a while. If you're in New York I'll come over for a few days and see you. We'll do Harlem.[1]

I'm working but it ain't much. I can't work here. Maybe no where any more as I once did. Once,— well, that was grand, anyway. Love,— Eddy,— as always.

Demuth

TO ALFRED STIEGLITZ

8 April 1929

Dear Stieglitz:—

I got your letter and Goodwin's check yesterday. Thanks,— for your part in that. It will look well with his others,— two others, I think he has, and it will have a nice home on 54th Street. So it's all right. Too, not many who could have afforded it would have liked it,— it not being peaches or flowers.

Am sending you back 300 by check which you can subtract

[1]The center of African-American nightlife had begun to shift to Harlem nearly a decade earlier because of the white craze for slumming in black speakeasies during what was then called the "negro renaissance."

from my Master account with you. Maybe I can do something about the Lachaise[1] thing too.

I think that I'll come over Sun. or Mon. to see the opening of the 100 American painters, and the Doves.[2] Will see you then. I wonder what the 100 show will look like. I'd love to get up an American show,— that is, if it were possible.

Love to Georgia & yourself,
Demuth

TO ALFRED STIEGLITZ
23 April 1929

Dear Stieglitz:—

I saw you the first night of the sale,[3] but could not find you afterwards. Mother came over the next day for two days and then I became ill, or something, and came home. Will tell you about that when I see you.

I 'phoned Lee [Simonson] and he said that he thought you could have the painting by this Saturday. Perhaps you had better call him,— I said that I would this week. Kraushaar[4] seemed delighted, I told him what you thought of doing.

I'll get the picture over to you by Saturday or Monday. Maybe I can bring them Sunday myself. When do you really want them. I hope & think I'm all right again, as nearly alright as I am these days.

Love,
Demuth

[1]French-American sculptor Gaston Lachaise.

[2]*One Hundred Important Paintings by Living American Artists,* Arts Council of the City of New York, Grand Central Palace, 15–27 April 1929.

[3]Emily Farnham's *Behind the Laughing Mask* lists the *Seventh Spring Salon Show,* 16 April–4 May 1929, as having included Demuth's work; Barbara Haskell's *Charles Demuth* (New York: Whitney Museum of American Art/Harry N. Abrams, 1987) does not.

[4]Gallery owner John Kraushaar.

TO ALFRED STIEGLITZ
9 May 1929

Dear Stieglitz:—

Last Monday, or Tues., I sent you some old drawings. I didn't think much of them, but they are all that remain of that period,— not, by the way, my blue period. One wasn't bad, as a drawing,— the one of Nana nude.[1]

On the book-shelves, under Georgia's portrait, are two tubes of vermillion paint. I forgot them,— they are wrapped in paper. Will you please send them to me,— sorry to bother you about this detail.

If Mrs. Norman[2] likes any of those drawings let her have them for what you think they are worth to her. You can return them to me,— or give them to Kraushaar. Have been gardening,— I have for the last three or four days, on this account, an awful pain in the back. Anyway, I haven't painted.

Love,
Demuth

TO ALFRED STIEGLITZ
13 August 1929

Dear Stieglitz:—

I wonder how you are? All right, I hope.

I've been here since seeing you,— and very low all summer,— so low that this is the first letter that I've written. Not even to Ettie [Stettheimer] who sent me a book months ago.

[1]Circa 1915–1918, Demuth executed a number of illustrations for books, including Zola's *Nana*.

[2]American writer and photographer Dorothy Norman, Stieglitz's companion. She co-edited *America and Alfred Stieglitz* (New York: Doubleday, 1934), which included Demuth's "Lighthouses and Fog," his tribute to his long-time mentor.

McBride was here for the Fourth,— three or four days.[1] I think he had a good time, but I did have an awful queer letter from him after his return! So maybe he didn't.

Have heard lots of things about and from Gertrude [Stein],— she may visit us soon. She seems to be telling that she has always been so interested in myself and work,— adding "but I've never seen any of Demuth's work,— he'd never show me any." She has great ideas about us all,— especially those she sees rarely. But thinks she must pay us a visit,— as American painting is all right and America, but not for her, or, she added, "Henry James." McBride & I on hearing all this decided that we'd go over my things in the autumn and select one,— and I'd send it to her as a surprise present,— and then see what she would do.

I've painted a bit and did a bit less writing. The "Creative Art" thing will be out in September,— at least the Sep. number is to have me in. I suppose that maybe will soon be out. Lee [Simonson] seems to be in Europe, as is most everyone else,— Eugene & C[arlotta Monterey O'Neill] having taken a chateau for 13 years,— not to have another "Dynamo" in it, I trust,— only love.

Is Georgia still in the Southwest? Give her my love when you write her. And Marsden [Hartley], is he about to cross or at the moment crossing? I know nothing about the world at the moment,— although most of my life has been given up to finding out about it,— perhaps I should have painted more! But I wasn't that interested in art.

Hope you've been well,— love my dear Stieglitz.

Demuth

[1]This was McBride's second visit to Lancaster, again for the Fourth of July holiday.

TO HENRY MCBRIDE

25 August 1929

Dear Henry:—

Mother is thanking you for the spoon, but it hasn't reached the kitchen. It's with the other spoons, and contented, I hope.

I hope you are again calm. Your letter, after your July visit, seemed unsettled. Do remember that Miss Gertrude has written after hers to Miss Dodge: "There is not all of any visit."[1]

Robert returned to us for the wedding, and seemed generally insulting,— not to us, however. I'm spending this week-end with him on the Island. "Come for a long weekend," said the command, "with Muriel [Draper]. We'll ruin you all in four days."[2] You better come along, otherwise you won't be safe.

Stieglitz writes that he has taken to flying, has gone to New York and back two or three times this summer, and has learned to run a motor-car, and there was something about golf! I really think Georgia should be informed. She I suppose will take up Indian something or other.

"Creative Art" writes that we will appear in the September number—about the 8th of September,— and adds, "the cuts of your paintings will appear without titles as they, the titles, did not reach London in time." Of course they did—or could have. I suppose they thought I was trying to ruin their magazine. I now wonder how they edited my few lines,— and yours—as we received no proofs![3]

And you think that "the Princess Z——" should be done.[4]

[1]Gertrude Stein's *Portrait of Mabel Dodge at the Villa Curonia,* the first work in her Cubist manner to be published, in 1912, and to receive wide public notoriety.

[2]The Lochers had taken a large house on Staten Island.

[3]For "Across a Greco Is Written."

[4]*The Princess Zoubaroff,* a 1920 play by the English fantasist Ronald Firbank about a community of nuns, lesbians, fey clerics, and effete English aristocracy swapping partners in Italy.

Well, I haven't read it. But if it is done I want Florine [Stettheimer] to do the sets, and I think Jerry should direct it, not Phil[1] nor Carl[2]—no, Jerry's the one.[3]

I suppose that corn is now in the pot. That's the end of all effort—the pot—after all the fussing,— our fussing. You will soon be returning to New York for the season, as will I, with luck.

Don't forget we have a date in the early season to pick Gertie a water-colour. I won't mention you, if you wish it kept quiet, in the presentation inscription. However, that can be worked out later.[4]

Best wishes for the remaining time at the farm.

Yours sincerely,
Charles

TO ALFRED STIEGLITZ
26 September 1929

Dear Stieglitz:—

Shall I pay these bills, or pay you? I'll do either. And thanks about "Creative Art." I too had a note from Dorothy Norman.[5]

[1]Philip Moeller, American playwright and director for the Theatre Guild.

[2]Carl Van Vechten had been Firbank's earliest advocate in the United States, writing about his work extensively, and Robert Locher had provided a frontispiece for Firbank's novel *Prancing Nigger,* 1924.

[3]American bon vivant Gerald Kelley, first an art dealer with the Braun Gallery, later employed by the Metropolitan Museum of Art.

[4]In *The Autobiography of Alice B. Toklas,* Stein accounts for a Demuth watercolor—"a remarkable little landscape in which the roofs and windows are so subtle that they are as mysterious and as alive as the roofs and windows of Hawthorne or Henry James"—having been left at her door in 1930 while she away. Its subsequent whereabouts has never been traced.

[5]Both Stieglitz and Norman had written to congratulate Demuth on his credo, published in *Creative Art.*

She seem[ed] pleased. I did think, from all the photographs he had which I gathered, he made a rather poor selection.[1] However,— I'm hoping that all together Henry [McBride] & myself made a few people angry.

About a week ago I returned from ten days in Atlantic City. It was grand,— so common, but no pretense that it isn't. I had a grand time. The exhibition of paintings which they have been holding during the summer was a surprise. It was quite good. And in the most beautiful gallery,— there is nothing in New York like those rooms. They sold a few things, and I think thousands saw the pictures. McBride sent some Marins and Mr. Phillips of Washington D.C. sent an O'Keeffe.[2] So we were all there,— except Dove and Florine [Stettheimer],— Florine who is Atlantic City when she's at top speed. They, I told them, should give Florine a whole show,— it would be wonderful. This brilliant idea of mine, however, did not make much of a hit.[3]

Bobby [Locher] took the poster with the white mask,— he said it was the only painting which touched Broadway,— & New York. I was so touched that I let him have it. It's still "unfinished,"— and he says that he will not allow me to work

[1]To illustrate "Across a Greco Is Written," Lee Simonson reproduced four paintings: two "untitled" watercolors, *Trees and Barns, Bermuda,* 1917 (of which Demuth penned a sketch at the foot of his letter to Stieglitz, 16 January 1924) and a flower piece; *Longhi on Broadway;* and the poster portrait of Georgia O'Keeffe, identified as "Poster in oil." It was followed by Henry McBride's generous essay, "Water-colours by Charles Demuth."

[2]Art patron Duncan Phillips, whose vast collection formed the nucleus of the Phillips Gallery in Washington, D.C.

[3]It is unlikely that Stettheimer would have agreed, had the offer been made. In 1916, Knoedler gave her a one-person exhibition; she sold no paintings, and subsequently refused to agree to another. She showed her paintings to her friends and occasionally entered pieces in joint shows.

on it, now that it's his.[1] But I shall really do Broadway, someday, with luck.

When are you coming down to town. Soon, I suppose, but it must be fine there now. I think that I'll go over around the 8th of October in about ten days.

Have some water-colours which I must show you before I put them out into the world,— poor things, the world is so strange. I wish that I didn't have to sell them. Not that I think they are so great,— but, well, you know.

Hope both G'Keeffe & you are well,— and to see you soon.

As ever,
Demuth

[1] *Design for a Broadway Poster.* This painting is often erroneously titled *Love, Love, Love (Hommage to Gertrude Stein)* on specious grounds that even a shallow familiarity with Stein's life and work contradicts. She had no connections with Broadway and only a casual acquaintance with Demuth; the suggestions that the mask in the painting has to do with her plays, and that the repetition of the word "love" reflects her celebrated "Rose is a rose is a rose is a rose," indicate a superficial knowledge of Stein's work. Locher's initial reaction to the painting, referred to here by Demuth, makes no mention of Stein. Stein and Demuth met in the winter of 1912–1913 and saw each other again in 1921, but so briefly that Stein forgot about it, according to *The Autobiography of Alice B. Toklas.* Demuth painted *Design for a Broadway Poster* five years before Stein's opera (with music by Virgil Thomson) *Four Saints in Three Acts* had a limited run in New York. There is no evidence that Demuth ever identified the painting with Gertrude Stein; Alfred Stieglitz did not exhibit it with this latter-day subtitle. According to Farnham (*Behind the Laughing Mask*), in 1956 Robert Locher and Richard Weyand said it was a poster portrait of Stein; so did Demuth's friend Susan Street. It remained in Locher's possession until his death; Edith Halpert of the Downtown Gallery then purchased it at auction as an untitled work. Farnham interviewed Street on 23 May 1956 and Halpert on 24 May 1956, after which Halpert assigned the Stein identification to it. See Frank, *Charles Demuth: Poster Portraits, 1923–1929.*

TO ALFRED STIEGLITZ
16 October 1929

Hotel Brevoort, Fifth Avenue at 8th Street
New York, New York

Dear Stieglitz:—

Again, New York. Again, this & that. Nothing really, but Helen Morgan.[1]

Those drawings, the ones I sent you for Mrs. Norman to look at,— didn't you say that you would send them to Kraushaar? They didn't amount to a great deal,— but the other day he said, "Haven't you some figure drawings (or water colours)?" "Those that came from Stieglitz last spring were the last & only," I told him. "But I didn't get any," he said. If you would let me know, here, perhaps I could get them. It doesn't really much matter, I suppose. Some one in Boston must have a drawing, it seems, of that vintage. The result of McBride chez "Creative Art," you know: "If there was only an acrobat drawing I'd take that." And if there was an acrobat drawing they'd want peaches. What most of them really need is a banana.

I hear that the Bliss-Crowninshield-Luxembourg—after its opening show of French—is to have a show of 15 living Americans![2] I don't think there are that many, myself,— but that's another matter again.

Love for you & Georgia.

As ever,
Demuth

[1]American popular singer Helen Morgan, then playing in *Show Boat,* the Jerome Kern–Oscar Hammerstein II musical version of Edna Ferber's novel.

[2]Lillie P. Bliss and Frank Crowninshield; the reference to Luxembourg is obscure. Demuth is referring to the initial exhibition, of French Impressionist and Post-Impressionist painting, at the Museum of Modern Art.

TO ALFRED STIEGLITZ
10 January 1930

Dear Stieglitz:—

Will you tell them for me at the Modern Museum that "My Egypt" is to come to you instead of going to Kraushaar.[1] I would have written Barr[2] but did not know his name. That is, tell them this if you really want that painting. It can be seen better with you than at the other place,— maybe [Duncan] Phillips will buy it.

Will you send me Barr's name and address some time. I must write him about something else.

Hope the Marins are going,— they looked so well.

Love,— as ever,
Demuth

TO JULIANA FORCE
14 January 1930

My dear Juliana:—

I'm writing to thank Mrs. Whitney[3] for the water-colour which she loaned me for the Modern Museum show. I hope it was returned to you in good condition.

I admired it several times myself while the show was going on,— fortunately, or unfortunately, one is only like that one summer of one's life!

Missed seeing you—you were in the country—when I was in

[1] *Paintings by Nineteen Living Americans* exhibition at the Museum of Modern Art, January 1930. Stieglitz planned a retrospective exhibition for April and May for Demuth, Dove, Hartley, and Marin in his new gallery, An American Place.
[2] Alfred Barr, Jr., Director of the Museum of Modern Art.
[3] Mrs John Hay Whitney.

to see you after your announcement in the "Times." Hope to have better luck, in a week or two, when again in town.

Best wishes for 1930.

Yours sincerely,
Charles Demuth

TO ALFRED STIEGLITZ[1]
12 October 1930

Hotel Brevoort, Fifth Avenue at 8th Street
New York, New York

Dear Stieglitz:

Am writing you from New York as you see. Was hoping to see you, but hear you will not be back until November.

Just couldn't write you before. Was not very well part of the summer, and then something else happened which almost finished me in another direction. So, all in all, my summer was one of the worst. However!!— here I am again back in New York, not much changed.

Didn't work at all, but have been again painting before I came to town for the last couple of weeks. Was going to bring what I've finished, one oil, along to show you but didn't, just as well now that I find you still in the country. You will see it next time I come over. I think you will like it. It's quite American, I think— no one will want it.

I saw McBride about three weeks ago at his place in the country. He had a grand short visit to Europe, seeing [*Stocktohn?*] and Gertrude [Stein] principally. Have seen also since here the new crop of art books on Americans and modern art. Not so hot. I feel like retiring from the world and doing one. Still if I did I suppose

[1]This letter is an edited transcription of a typewritten version made by Barbara Haskell.

I could never go out again. McBride told me that DuBois[1] is constantly writing him blaming all his troubles on him. I think his one and only trouble is that he's a very bad painter.

There are some pictures showing their faces in New York. Nothing much that I've seen. Will look them over again tomorrow.

I went to see Barnes at my worst this summer. He was in Europe. But Mme. Barnes received me as of old. He probably gave instructions. Will try to pay him a visit soon as I hear he is back.

Will see you soon, give my love to Georgia, and tell her I still think she is good, without any, if, or, but. With love to you, Stieglitz

Sincerely,
Demuth

TO ALFRED STIEGLITZ
17 January 1931

With these go a movement of flames. Flame of the spirit? Flame of the flesh?— perhaps the flame, only, of creation; however, it consumes,— that is success in a flame. Sometimes it burns vermillion, sometime[s] it burns emeraude with violet edgings, but it always burns and moves. Moves at times like great flames fanned by great winds from the sea, at other times like things burn in-doors, as candles behind the elevated Host. At times like the electric arch; then, the movement and the colour seem not to be movement and colour anymore,— the movement being that slight rest before any consumation which is supreme movement, or balance, and the colour being some colour beyond those we see.

[1]French expatriate Urban Realist painter Guy Pène DuBois.

This is part of something being done for Georgia;[1] as it will never be done, perhaps you had better have this,— as I'm rather pleased with this fragment. Hope you will be,— see you during show.

C. Demuth

TO ALFRED STIEGLITZ
17 February 1931

Dear Stieglitz:—

Would have written you before but grippe has been raging in the home.

Everything is all right with me about the same to Mrs. H[are].—would have been glad for the 775—had a letter from her since, and she seems to be delighted. So,— many thanks.

Mrs. Force took, if I understand it, "My Egypt"—haven't the money as yet so maybe I don't understand it. You will get the "Pears" in a day or two. The price was not so bad—or very good. Still it will have a home and it was one of my good things.

If you still have that photograph of the "Calla Lilies"—I think I left it there, on the table when in New York, I forgot it—give it to Kootz,[2] please. I don't think that I can have the "Figure 5" photographed here. I'll write him—as I sent him the photograph you did of me, yesterday. I hope they don't ruin it.

Am working—may see you some weekend soon. Hope Georgia is better and that her show is going.

Love,
Demuth

[1]Stieglitz did not use all of this section of Demuth's long-gestating "Three" in the catalog for an O'Keeffe exhibition. It is impossible to determine how much of this essay Demuth wrote circa 1926 when he first embarked on "Three," some of which was used for an earlier catalog, and how much of it he wrote later.

[2]American art critic Samuel L. Kootz, author of *Modern American Painters,* which included information about Demuth. He later gave a Stieglitz portrait of Demuth to the Museum of Modern Art.

TO ALFRED STIEGLITZ

7 March 1931

Dear Stieglitz:—

I was about to bring the "Figure 5" painting over to you today, Saturday, by motor, but my nose started to run. So that movement was off.

However, have expressed it to Of,— it should be there today or Monday,— could you or Georgia look it over when it is unpacked and see that it made the trip properly. If not I'll have to come over and again fix it up. I sent two over, in fact, the big still-life with the masks [*Longhi on Broadway*],— this I ask Of to send over to you.[1] I hope nothing happens to them. But—you know!

I'll bring the others over by motor sometime this month, later. I did want very much to bring the one for Kootz,— as I could have been careful of it,— but I couldn't make it.

Barnes has been going wild in Philadelphia, I hear—will tell you all those pretty details when I see you. For real madness this story gets the prize.

Mrs. [Edith] Halpert seems pleased about it all. And writes me from time to time—since the sale—telling me that she's sold some and this morning that she is arranging a show: "Seven masters of water-colour."[2] Of course I think there is only one,— still, what do I know of the art world. I can only tell when I'm moved. Pictures don't move me often and living moves me too often,— so what can I know of seven masters of water-colour?— still.

See you soon, I hope. Love to you & Georgia.

Demuth

[1]Stieglitz was mounting a Demuth exhibition at An American Place for March, to be followed by a group show, including Demuth, Dove, Hartley, Marin, and O'Keeffe, *Masters of Water Colour,* 16–30 March 1931.

[2]Downtown Gallery, 29 May–12 July 1931.

TO ALFRED STIEGLITZ

10 September 1931

Dear Stieglitz:—

Will write you, as I've been intending to do, for weeks, at once, an hour after reading your letter.

My summer,— well, it's almost over and as I realize this fact I also realize that most of it found me numb. I've gardened and I've sun-burned myself—and maybe I've painted. I think, really, my summer's painting—only one—is all right. I think that you will like it too. It's an oil. And seems more to the point than most,— different, I feel. Perhaps I'm just, in my suffering, making myself feel this,— from my others. Anyway it has a grand name—it's called "And the Land of the Brave."[1]

I haven't written much—I wanted that thing which we talked about and which I told you I had started to be very light, anyway on its surface,— and I have not felt that way for months. I saw what Marsden did about Miss Florine[2] after which I did a little on what I've done about her![3]

Too, I've finished reading the final book of the Proust sufferings. Most of it is like my big Marin water-colour: it doesn't quite happen, but the idea being so grand,— well, you are quite satisfied with what is there.[4] Of course the pages which do "happen" are quite like the water-colours when they "happen," in and beyond Time.

No, I haven't been paid by Mrs. W[ertheim]. If I were only as

[1]Later, Demuth altered this title to *And the Home of the Brave.* Charles Daniel, with whom Demuth had broken off relations entirely, still admired his watercolors, but on July 17 Daniel wrote to Ferdinand Howald that he thought "in his oils he is straining to do what [Oscar] Blumner does with very much more power, spirit and imagination."

[2]"The Paintings of Florine Stettheimer," *Creative Art,* July 1931.

[3]"Florine Stettheimer" in *Three,* 1998.

[4]*Cliffs and Sea,* 1926.

well off as they think, I'd give them away. At that I almost, it seems, do!

Tell Georgia I have a letter started for her,— it's been so for months,— maybe she will receive it some day. It's nice to know that you are still going on,— I am too. Will see you in New York. Until then, my love for you & Georgia.

Demuth

TO ALFRED STIEGLITZ

28 April 1932

Dear Stieglitz:—

Here is the five.[1] Forgive me for not sending it sooner.

Tell Georgia that I'll be over to take her to the opening of the new museum. I haven't received a notice of its opening, so maybe she had better let me know when it is to be.[2]

Love.

As ever,
Demuth

TO ALFRED STIEGLITZ

23 October 1932

Dear Stieglitz:—

Will you please put the enclosed ticket on that oil painting of mine,— the new one in the black frame, the one with the blue

[1]He refers to *I Saw the Figure Five in Gold.* Stieglitz was mounting an impromptu exhibition in May of his now established stable of five artists: Demuth, Dove, Hartley, Marin, and O'Keeffe. This marked the last time that Stieglitz exhibited Demuth's work.

[2]The Museum of Modern Art. Demuth, O'Keeffe, ballet impresario Lincoln Kirstein, and Carl Van Vechten went to the opening of the Musem of Modern Art.

sky and yellow water-tower,[1] and let it go down to the Whitney Museum along with Georgia's.

I hoped to attend to it myself,— but got to feeling rather badly when I was in New York and came home without seeing you, and [have] been laid up ever since with pains in my hip,— but not in my lame leg hip. It's all very strange and trying.

I wonder how Georgia is holding up.

If possible will come over soon,— maybe for the opening of the Museum's American Show. Do want to see how Georgia and myself look in a show with Whistler's "Mother."

All my mail for the past week have been request[s], for some, or it would seem, of my much desired paintings. I wish some one would really desire one to the extent of spending some money.

Give my love to O'Keeffe, and I send you some too.

Yours,
Demuth

TO JULIANA FORCE
28 September 1933

[telegram]
Lancaster, Pennsylvania

RECEIVED NO INVITATION LET ME KNOW ABOUT SHOW[2] HAVE NEW WATER COLORS HERE BEST REGARDS

DEMUTH

[1]Demuth may be referring to either *And the Home of the Brave,* 1931, or *Buildings, Abstractions Lancaster,* 1931. Both have blue skies; one has a red water tower and the other has black water towers; one has a yellow sign and the other has a yellow chimney. In October 1932, paintings done in 1931 were not "new," but no later painting fits Demuth's description either.

[2]Probably the A. E. Gallatin Collection, with a catalog published by New York University, *Gallery of Living Art,* containing reproductions of four Demuth works: Zola's *L'Assommoir,* 1918, *In Vaudeville,* 1918, *Zinnias,* 1921, and *Peaches,* 1923; the last three were donated to the Philadelphia Museum of Art.

TO JULIANA FORCE
1 November 1933

My dear Juliana:—

I have two water-colours, new ones, painted this summer of flowers here in Lancaster,— would rather leave these in show than those older ones which you can see at Kraushaar's.

Shall I send these on to you and when? Or shall I send them to Kraushaar and you can see them there.

Hoping that you are as always when I've seen you,— well, and, to see you soon, with love.

As ever,
Demuth

TO FISKE KIMBALL[1]
postmark 15 December 1933

My dear Mr. Kimball:—

In answer both to your wire & letter concerning the meeting at the [Philadelphia] Museum regarding the needy artist, I don't believe that Lancaster Co. has any artists, needy or otherwise.

I'm afraid most of us are farmers,— I think I'm the only one probably in the county foolish enough to have gone in for so called art.

However, if there is anything that I can do I would be glad to help. Or, if any help is needed of which I happen to hear I will inform you.

[1]Director of the Philadelphia Museum of Art.

Having been laid up for some time I was not able to attend meeting.

Yours sincerely,
C. Demuth

TO ALFRED STIEGLITZ

1 February 1934

Am writing to you, as Georgia said she might go back Wed. I'll come over Monday the 5th for a few days. Tried to come this week to see her and pictures but had a cold and many other troubles. Anyway love to you both.

Yours,
Demuth

TO ROBERT S. JOSEPHY[1]

[circa 24 June 1934]

My dear Mr. Josephy:—

There is nothing that I would like more than to see my drawings in a book with the James story.

But,— the drawings are no longer mine. They belong to Philip Goodwin whom Mr. Stieglitz will tell where you can reach, in New York, but I do not have address. If you get in touch with Goodwin and he says that it is alright I shall be delighted.

[1]American book designer with Harcourt Brace and Company. This attempt followed Edna Kenton's in 1924. See page 65, footnote 2.

I don't want any money. Anyway the drawings are not mine. It will all depend on what Goodwin wishes to do about it.

You can see all the drawings at Goodwin's.

I do hope it can be arranged.

Yours sincerely,
C. Demuth

P.S. There [are] four drawings for "The Turn of the Screw."

C. D.

TO ROBERT S. JOSEPHY
[circa 29 June 1934]

My dear Josephy:—

Mr. Frank Osborn, #1, 5th Ave., owns, or did own, those drawings. Suppose you call him,— or write him as I'm afraid he has already gone away for the summer.

I'm sure Osborn will settle all our troubles.[1]

Yours,
C. Demuth

[1]Josephy wrote to Osborn, but his reply, if any, has not survived; nor was Demuth's desire to see his illustrations published with *The Turn of the Screw* ever realized. After writing this letter, Demuth went to Provincetown with Frank and Elsie Everts for the summer and there executed twelve paintings and drawings in a sketchbook; they were the last work he completed. Although he lived another year, there is no documentation to indicate that he ever left home again after he returned to Lancaster in the fall. Demuth had hoped to return to Paris the following year, with Frank and Elsie Everts, ostensibly to illustrate Proust's *À la recherche du temps perdu,* the eight-volume novel he had read in installments as it was issued in translation during the 1920s.

TO ALFRED STIEGLITZ
[circa 1934–1935?]

Dear Mr. Stieglitz:—

You will get by express, sometime today, the toad which Hartley has spoken to you about,[1] and which I would like you to have for a month or two. You will like it, I think.

Yrs sincerely,
C. Demuth[2]

[1]Marsden Hartley gave Demuth a Mayan toad, carved in stone, as a souvenir of his 1932 trip to Mexico. It resided on the hearth in the dining room at 118 East King Street until Demuth sent it to Stieglitz. Demuth's mother, Augusta, left instructions with her will that the toad was to be given to Alfred C. and Lilia Barnes; Mrs. Barnes collected toads to populate her garden. It is now in the permanent collection of the Barnes Foundation.

[2]This is Charles Demuth's last letter to have survived. Severely weakened by his long illness, he contracted dropsy, then arterial sclerosis, and died in his sleep on 23 October 1935. His mother Augusta died in 1943. In accordance with her son's wishes, she willed to Robert Locher the circa 1770 house at 118 East King Street, where the Demuth family had lived since 1883. At some point, perhaps after her husband's death in 1911, Augusta Demuth rented out the first floor front space of the house for commercial use; she and her son had occupied the second floor and both floors of the adjacent wing that extended out into the extensive garden behind. Subsequently, Locher and his companion Richard Weyand operated an antique shop in the first floor front space and a clothing shop in the second floor front space; they resided in the rest of the house. On Locher's death in 1956, the property passed to Weyand. After Weyand's death later that year, the house was sold at auction, and then the entire space was renovated for commercial use; the garden and its elaborate brick walks were paved over for parking space. In 1981, the Demuth Foundation was established; it opened to the public in November 1983 on the centennial anniversary of Charles Demuth's birth, with the garden and back wing of the house restored as a museum. In 1986, the Foundation acquired the house next-door at 116 East King Street, belonging to Dorothea Demuth, the widow of Charles's cousin Christopher. This includes the first tobacco shop in America, still in continuous operation since 1770, at 114 East King Street; the first snuff mill, built over a period of time at the rear of the property, beginning in 1798; and a tobacco manufactory, built in 1859. The Demuth Foundation now preserves this family enclave and operates a museum and study center devoted to the work of Charles Demuth. It includes a number of artifacts associated with his life and more than two dozen examples of his immarcescible art.

AN APPRECIATIVE APPENDIX

At least seven of Charles Demuth's contemporaries championed his work in print while he was alive, and an eighth one shortly after his death. Art critic Henry McBride began writing about Demuth in 1914—with qualified interest—in the *New York Sun* and later for the periodical *Creative Art*. He concluded—in admiration—with a review of the Demuth memorial exhibition at the Whitney Museum in 1937. Willard Huntington Wright—who later, as S. S. Van Dyne, invented the mystery sleuth Philo Vance—wrote about Demuth's work in *International Studio* in 1917. Helen Henderson, one of Demuth's fellow students at the Pennsylvania Academy of the Fine Arts, later became art critic for the *Philadelphia Inquirer* and in 1918 published a fulsome assessment of her friend's work. Novelist and cultural maven Carl Van Vechten wrote an appreciation in 1922 for the literary journal *Reviewer*. Art critic and collector Albert E. Gallatin wrote about Demuth in his book *American Water-Colourists* in 1922, and five years later he produced a book devoted solely to the artist's work, *Charles Demuth*. In 1931, art critic Angela E. Hagen offered a long review and Demuth's early friend Rita Wellman a memoir, both for *Creative Art*. In 1936, Marsden Hartley published an autobiographical fragment, part of which served as a eulogy for his friend and fellow painter. Selections from these writings are arranged here in chronological order to indicate the published response to Demuth's work during his lifetime and immediately after his death. They have been edited to correct typographical errors, to make the selections consistent in matters of form, to supply missing information, and to excise impertinent or extraneous material.

WHAT IS HAPPENING IN THE WORLD OF ART

by Henry McBride, New York Sun, 1 November 1914

It is Charles Demuth who now makes his debut in the Daniel Gallery. He exhibits twenty-five aquarelles,[1] which are washed in with great freedom and are in pretty color, but whose landscape subjects are sometimes so vaguely indicated as to be practically negligible. This drawback will not puzzle that portion of the public which has learned to admire the faint color evocations of John Marin, but then it must be confessed that this portion of the public is the scared minority not numerous enough as yet to dare to raise the voice of praise.

John Marin's "indicated" water colors are not more elusive than many of Whistler's most popular pastels, but then Whistler went further upon occasions into completed portraits that anybody could recognize to be likenesses, and these could be rushed to the defence by the Whistler enthusiast, when attacked. Marin laughs at likenesses and defies you to recognize the particular hill or particular bridge. For that matter it is seldom that he even admits it is "a bridge." In consequence his followers get into dif-

[1]Watercolors; the popularity of the medium canceled out common usage of its French equivalent circa 1915.

ficulties when proselyting for him, and are sometimes called "highbrows." Nevertheless, their number increases steadily.

For them the question will not be "Is Mr. Demuth too vague?" but "Is he sufficiently different from Marin?"

This present exhibition does not answer with sufficient distinctness. It will be allowed that Mr. Demuth's drawings are worthy of exhibition and that they have merit enough to induce us to hope that this artist will do still better. He has at his present command a good but not extraordinary sense of color. His drawing is uncertain and in consequence the waters in some of his seascapes travel up and down over a too concave earth. This might be forgivable if the color had been sought for in passionate subtleties, but the color is only "good"; and if the lines as lines had relationships to an idea worth expressing, but they are not concerned with ideas, and so as drawing must be rated "weak."

An amusing and novel feature of Mr. Demuth's show is the extreme simplicity of his catalogue. Six of the aquarelles are labelled with the same title, "Trees," five are called "Dunes" and five "The Bay." Two are called "Conestoga." We have a vague notion that "Conestoga" is somewhere in Pennsylvania and that therefore our artist is a Quaker.[1] In that case he will be more than ever worth watching, for he must be revolutionary, his sense of color being already beyond what we expect from a Hicksite.

DEMUTH

by Henry McBride, New York Sun, 3 December 1916

Charles Demuth's assets as an artist are: A delightful color sense, a delicate and rare sort of humor and a command over flowing line.

[1]The Conestoga is a minor tributary, in Lancaster, of the Susquehanna River. Demuth was a member of Trinity Lutheran Church.

He is showing a number of his new water colors in the Daniel Galleries. [. . .] There are some watercolors of Mr. Demuth that have not been hung upon the walls. The subjects were suggested by a reading of Zola's *Nana.* They are kept hidden in a portfolio, and are only shown to museum directors and proved lovers of modern art upon presentation of visiting cards. They are quite advanced. [. . .]

THE UNDERGROUND SEARCH FOR HIGHER MORALITIES

by Henry McBride, New York Sun, 25 November 1917

Charles Demuth is being an artist, as Miss Gertrude Stein would say. His water colors in the Daniel Galleries are a distinct success. Mr. Demuth is a friend of Miss Stein's. Therefore *The Sun* begs in Nimes, in the south of France, "to please copy" that Mr. Demuth is a success. Miss Stein is in Nimes. "She and Alice [Toklas]," so writes a friend, "left Paris on the 9th in their little Ford car for Nimes to establish a post there and distribute aid to the hospitals and colonies of refugees. They have done splendid work and done it in lovely places. That's all right—they might as well be in a nice place as in a horrid one.

But perhaps Miss Stein knows it already. There is something peculiarly occult about success. It has methods of its own for getting itself wirelessly about. How else could all of those people who were at the press view have known of it? Why, even Brother Montross was there, and you know things are getting pretty serious when a dealer visits a rival dealer's shop! It is time to protest, however, against these encroachments on the almost obsolete press view. Critics are after all only human beings and such as their poor thoughts are they have to collect them after their fashion. To have people pulling you by the elbow and saying, "Isn't this one wonderful?" and "No, you can't have that one, it's already sold," is enough to arouse the Lord Northcliffe that is usually dormant in the most amiable bosom. But in spite of all this temptation to discover flaws in Mr. Demuth's art, none after a thorough search could be found.

It is also pleasant to record that this artist, who is a cubist nor' by nor'west; that is to say, only occasionally, is more of a cubist than ever when the wind blows nor' by nor'west! Cubism is so useful in infuriating the philistines that it would be a pity to have it halt even in a time like this, when infuriating the philistines is not so uppermost in the minds of Christians as it once was. But be assured the philistines are not resting upon their oars [. . .] and it is up to all true artists—bravo, Mr. Demuth—to bear aloft the banner with the strange device. Sincerity, seriousness, genuineness, inventiveness, fantasy are fine things, even when cubistic. It is all the more joy to have them, when put cryptically, puzzle those of little faith. It is one way of sifting out the sinners.

[. . .] Another quality that I should have put into Mr. Demuth's list is humor. His studies of downstairs restaurants and upstairs vaudevillists are tinged with wit. I don't know why it is, but the moment you go down-stairs into a restaurant in New York you begin to see life. Or so I judge from Mr. Demuth's drawings. How revolting, for instance, must not have been "Baron Wilk[in]s's" establishment? It has been closed by the police some time since. Races of various colors intermingled, danced and drank there. Yet I hold it was entirely right of Mr. Demuth to have studied it, so evidently in the interests of higher morality. What excuses young Mr. Duchamp and young Mr. Fisk can offer for descending into such resorts I cannot image. They may say they went along to protect Mr. Demuth in the performance of his duty, but in that case surely it was unnecessary for Mr. Fisk to place his arm quite so caressingly about the colored lady with whom he is taking wine in the picture. It is all very well for the great Baudelaire to do such things but in

America there is an entirely different conception of what is and what is not permissible. Perhaps Mr. Fisk will say that his arm composes better in that position, but I reject that explanation also as inadequate. As a possible future contributor to the *Art World* I candidly confess that the view of Baron Wilks's restaurant—charming as it is in color, movement, atmosphere, &c.—alarms me.

Less disconcerting are two water colors inspired by Henry James's grewsome tale, "The Turn of the Screw." They will doubtless have the effect of putting all Washington Square to a rereading of that uncanny story. Henry James himself would rub his eyes could he but see them. They are like a translation into French and a translation into French is a process that helps mysteries. [. . .] James becomes refined. Edward Fitzgerald confessed once that he never could read Poe in the original. It was too raw for his taste. He was obliged to take it through the medium of Baudelaire. I've had the same feeling in regard to James, [. . .] so I will end this at once by saying that if Mr. Demuth will only effect some further translations from this admired writer I shall regard it as putting a personal obligation upon myself.

DEMUTH

by Willard Huntington Wright, International Studio, 4 December 1917

At the Daniel Gallery are to be seen the oils of [Edward] Fisk and the watercolours of Charles Demuth. Demuth's pictures constitute, for me, the most important modern show of the month. The painter had made great strides since last he showed his work, especially in his landscapes, which are charming as Picasso's early oils of the same type. In Demuth's figure pieces and scenes of circus and music-hall folk is much that is Picasso, and a great deal that is Toulouse-Lautrec. [. . .]

The unfortunate thing about Demuth's work is that it reveals in the artist a contentment with his tricks and mannerisms, and a lack of striving for more solid and masculine attributes. Occasionally, however, there are real balances of volume, as, for instance in the pictures of the ballet girl on horseback. And Demuth has a real feeling for complete color scales.

At bottom, of course, he is a draughtsman who reinforces his drawings with colour, and not an aquarellist at all, as is Marin. But, it is to be hoped this painter, in the near future, will devote his entire time to organizing his sensations, not into interesting illustrations, but into aesthetically moving pictures. Already he is beginning to grapple with the deeper problems of aesthetics.

from ART AND ARTISTS PASS IN REVIEW

by Helen Henderson, Philadelphia Inquirer, 1 December 1918

Recent watercolors by Charles Demuth occupy the rarified atmosphere of the Daniel Gallery, New York, until December 14. "Recent water colors by Demuth, of Lancaster." The announcement augurs well for a congenial atmosphere, especially if the visitor has been sated previously with big, general exhibitions of water colors. At all events, stepping from the life, which passes in its brief ascent Elsie de Wolffe's domain, and leaving the sharp bark of the actress decorator's red-haired spaniel in the nether regions, the advance through glass portals, as into a conservatory is well followed up by the aspect of the clean, crisp Daniel Gallery, behung with seventy-one clear, crystal expressions from a naif mind.

We of Philadelphia are so ready to discount the performance of a local prophet, and Mr. Demuth himself is so utterly devoid of the professional bluff—the so-called swelled head—that one always feels that his exquisite art should be, in a sense, rubbed in as much as possible, in speaking to Philadelphians.

Philadelphia bred him, it is true—he grew up in the Philadelphia Academy schools under Anshutz, and under that sympathetic master, at Fort Washington. I can remember the junior instructor calling him down for what was meant for salutary contempt for "feeling" his art, for discussing "emotion" in painting. "I don't so feel it" used to be quite a phrase with us—a phrase which Anshutz accepted and dealt with, but which the other masters resented bitterly. I think Joe de Camp[1] started this crusade against our finer feelings. He tried to bring our study down to something about as actual as a photograph, and, since Joe was a draughtsman, according to the legitimate academic way of thinking, he was allowed to set a pace.

Now that Demuth has "arrived"—has made more than good, we see nothing of his work in Philadelphia—occasionally a water color from his hand might get into the annual exhibit of works in that medium, but if the jury took it the Hanging Committee took care so to place it that it would be the last thing seen if seen at all. Top line in the corridor was its place. Meanwhile Charles never did more than laugh an amused chuckle at his rating and paint away contentedly whenever he felt the call—either in his province or in Bermuda or on Cape Cod, at Provincetown.

And for now, I think, four Novembers Mr. Daniel has devoted his gallery to an annual display. There is something very personal about this gallery. It is not for hire—nothing is shown there that the host does not stand for personally. So there is a kind of standard and, above all, a warm sense of hospitality about the place.

We are to think of Mr. Demuth now as Mr. Daniel's guest and there is a fine sense of rapport between the two.

The work this year divides itself into three groups or kinds. The most recent expression of the artist's mind is to be found in the larger group of "New England Houses"; his rare sense of

[1]American Realist painter Joseph Rodefer De Camp.

beauty is revealed in his group of "Flowers," while his delicious humor and grasp of essential essence comes out in four illustrations in color done for Henry James's *The Turn of the Screw*.

To one who has appreciated the true flavor of Provincetown and Cape Cod, Demuth's "New England Houses" will make their subtle appeal. One must take them, of course, as poetic transcriptions—dreams, souvenirs, memories of the gables and windows, the piled-up roofs, of these elementary buildings, the product of the housewright—never of the architect. Architecture is unknown in Provincetown—thank God—at least it was until the beach combers began to take themselves seriously.

New England houses of the typical kind—and that is the kind Demuth has found inspiring—are all hung from the ridge pole. The peak is sharp to afford a swift descent for falling snow. Whatever color they may be painted, the sun and salt air soon makes it beautiful.

Demuth has been quaintly amused by the red house with its white margins—its outlined windows. He particularly delights in the end chimneys, in the peaked ends piled artlessly as by a child upon the slope of a drumlin. Really, the longer one lingers, especially if he have the memory of the reality to enrich his vision, the more one feels that whatever these houses may mean, Demuth got from their contemplation a deeply personal thrill, and, however vague his impressions may be, measured by the Joe de Camp sort of standard, the literal photography of such a leader as, let us say, Tarbell[1]—still there is in them the spirit or the soul, what you will, of the New England houses, and from these accounts of them one can build up an intimate knowledge of the whole village, country, peninsula.

Of "Flowers" Mr. Demuth makes eight very beautiful drawings. "Quality" seems to be the attribute which predominates in

[1]American Impressionist painter Edmund Charles Tarbell.

their handling. The artist chooses certain themes, such as the pink wild orchid, and introduces it into his picture with a charming reticence—a marvellous tact. The pink wild orchid enters into a composition as a charming maiden enters into her mother's drawing-room. The setting is prepared for just such sweet intrusion—she fits exquisitely—she is dainty, shy, elusive, yet she dominates delicately the entire situation—every circumstance is subdued to her pitch, everything fine in her entourage comes to the surface.

Other flowers get the same sympathetic treatment—one cannot recall distinctly what they are. There is a delicious blue reverie of larkspur or delphinium and a particularly pleasing combination of something fragile and delicate with soft, gray pine-cones of a past season. Now these pine-cones again bespeak the true companion of the Cape. They have the silver quality of old shingles. The tree that bears them has bent before many a wintry blast, has held its ground before searching sand blasts, has harbored many a snow-drift. Perchance it has been one of a buried forest—disclosed in picturesque ruin after centuries of oblivion.

For the sands of the Cape move with incredible velocity and where nature's barriers have given way or been destroyed by the ruthless cutting of trees or cutting of beach grass—vast areas of forest have been gradually submerged. It is all this which gives romantic interest to the Cape. And something of it all comes back, even in New York, in the color and shape of these pine-cones.

The catalogue lists only the four illustrations for *The Turn of the Screw,* but there are three others in the show. Demuth's "Vaudeville" has always supreme humor. He gives us in the present drawing a genial, bold individual playing a sort of viola, which he holds as though it were a 'cello between his spare knees, but resting on the seat of his chair. His face is suffused by a peculiar white blush which mounts upward from the gills and threatens to engulf his physiognomy in impenetrable mist. There is something supernatural about it but the performer rises above it, as it were, and exhibits a gnarled cranium that alone is worth the price of admission.

One illustration for *The Masque of the Red Death* is an eloquent tale of fantastic fate and *The Beach* has the charm of that series.

The four drawings for James's story are elusive and difficult to write about. They show rich imagination, have none of the vulgar, obvious attributes—here and there "quality" gives way to a naif technique, but usually quality is supreme and forms the chief charm.

from FLORINE STETTHEIMER AND CHARLES DEMUTH

by Carl Van Vechten, Reviewer, February 1922

Edgar Saltus once remarked: "America is in the matter of art as it is in the matter of truffles: we consume but we do not produce." This is a good epigram but it is not altogether true. Any country which has produced Herman Melville, Henry James, James McNeill Whistler, James Branch Cabell, Joseph Hergesheimer, and Edgar Saltus himself cannot be held entirely contemptible in the matter of art.[1] Art of various percentages is distilled everywhere, even, perhaps, in New Jersey, but usually there is little appreciation for home-brews. We prefer expensive importations. It is easy to sell a picture for $50,000 in America whether the picture is worth it or not. The sale is of sufficient importance to be recorded in the newspapers and the buyer proves, merely by hanging the picture on his wall, not only that he is a man of culture but also that he is a man of position and property. His might be called Rolls-Royce snobbery. But it is a difficult and ticklish matter to put a contemporary

[1]Ironically, in 1922, Melville and Saltus were largely forgotten, while the now forgotten Cabell and Hergesheimer (along with Van Vechten himself) were among the most successful novelists of the period.

American canvas up for sale at $50,000. The dealers, indeed, by the very force of circumstances, are compelled to ask comparatively small prices for such canvases. The possessor of one of these, therefore, can only be called a man of courage. Some of his friends, doubtless, remark that he bought it because it was cheap.

I wonder how many collectors are buying the water-colours of Charles Demuth? In a few years they will surely bring big prices. Have you seen his jugglers and acrobats and circus clowns, his flowers, and his illustrations for *Nana* and *The Turn of the Screw?* The sketches for Henry James's necromantic tale are stranger than the tale itself. They do not reveal; they conceal. They keep the secret of the master in a decorative manner. On the other hand, the illustrations for *Nana,* elaborate in realistically fanciful arabesques the vicious horrors of Zola. How beautiful and how terrible the flowers: daisies with cabalistic secrets, cyclamens rosy with vice, orchids wet with the mystery of the Rosicrucians! And the acrobats, the jugglers, and the clowns all contribute their share to the glory of this perverse genius, a genius which would be recognized at once at full-value in Germany or France. His later pictures, apparently depicting houses in New England villages are orderly and concrete, and yet . . .

from AMERICAN WATER-COLOURISTS

by A. E. Gallatin (New York: E. P. Dutton, 1922)

With Cézanne came a new tradition for the painter in water-colour, a freshness and a transparency which did not hitherto exist. Came also from this great innovator, one of the most notable in the history of painting, profound studies of plastic relations and of significant forms, suggested with the most sensitive washes of exquisite colour and "realized" (to employ a term often used by the painter) more often than in the paintings in oil. In a general way it is to this tradition that belong the water-colours of John Marin and Charles Demuth, who have built up their drawings in much the same spirit as did Cézanne, and the Chinese before him, not caring merely for the purely graphic appearance of nature, the superficial aspect. [. . .]

Charles Demuth, with respect to the subjects of his water-colours, is one of the most versatile of the American masters of the medium: this gifted artist has made studies of flowers, views of factories and other buildings, landscape interpretations, illustrations for various works of fiction, and studies of vaudeville performers. All are conceived and executed in a very modern spirit. Demuth, who was born and who lives in Lancaster, Pennsylvania, receiving his school at the Pennsylvania Academy, is another aquarellist whose work is essentially American in feeling.

Demuth's talent is confined within very definite limits; his drawings are always conspicuous of their perfect taste and a certain daintiness which amounts at times almost to fastidiousness. His drawings of flowers (he has also made one of a Japanese orange tree) are exquisite, full of the most delicate draughtsmanship and alluring colour. Style they possess, as well as something of the subtle charm one finds in the flower subjects of Redon and Fantin-Latour. In the rendering of flowers no other American has equalled him. Demuth's drawings of buildings, usually made at Provincetown, Massachusetts, or Coatesville, Pennsylvania,[1] are full of the locality of the scene.

For Zola's *Nana* Demuth has made seven or eight illustrations; for Henry James's *The Turn of the Screw* four; for a book by Wedekind, a modern German dramatist, seven;[2] for Poe's *The Masque of the Red Death* a single drawing, as he has for Balzac's

[1]Demuth did only two paintings of Coatesville sites: *Incense of a New Church,* 1921, and *The End of the Parade,* 1922; the others were of Lancaster locales. Gallatin repeated his error in his 1927 *Charles Demuth.*

[2]Frank Wedekind's play *Erdgeist.*

The Girl of the Golden Eyes; while three were drawn for Henry James's *The Beast in the Jungle.* These water-colours are full of imagination and display consummate artistry; it is regrettable that only a few of them have been published, for no American has done quite such distinguished work in this direction. As works of art, in distinction to their illustrative value, these water-colours possess an importance such as attaches to the decorative illustrations of Aubrey Beardsley, the greatest master of black and white the world has known since Dürer and Holbein. One scents in these drawings of Demuth a certain admiration for the lithographs of Toulouse-Lautrec, as one does also in the fifty or sixty acrobat and other vaudeville drawings which the artist has made. Beside possessing Lautrec's love for the theatre and the circus, we find in Demuth's drawings unusual but perfectly balanced compositions, a line which is alive and vital, and colour harmonies of rare beauty—all qualities also common in the great Frenchman. Rumour has it that Demuth may make a set of drawings for a volume dealing with the great vaudeville artists which Marsden Hartley is said to contemplate writing: what a delightful book this would be!

DEMUTH

by Henry McBride, New York Sun, 10 April 1926

No greater contrast to the art of John Marin could be asked for than that is supplied by Charles Demuth and which is exhibited now in the Intimate Gallery where Marin lately held forth. Marin grows more and more passionate, more tempestuous and nervous. The opposing currents of modern life seem to beat in upon his spirit relentlessly. He feels each jerky, jazz like force that comes along and, to the death, must translate it into rhythms. He is another melancholy Dane who says "Oh cursed spite," but always in the end accepts the challenge and wars it out with nature to tragic though triumphant conclusions.

Demuth, with the aid of science, doubtless wraps himself in some sort of a transparent cloak and shields himself from the contrary winds. He is like these deep sea experts who sink beneath the waves incased in glass, to come back when the supply of oxygen has been exhausted with reports of wonders. Not a ripple from the upper airs is allowed to disturb the intensity of his study. If a storm rages he will hear about it from Marin afterward. But this scientifically induced calm is by no means stagnation. There is life to be observed from the spot where he has taken up his station and, since science secures you from fogs, he gets it straight.

Physicists, consequently, will block the entrance to the Intimate Gallery, struggling to get at the color facts of the matter. Demuth is the one who hands them out. To me he is more reliable than Chevruel.[1] But, then, Chevruel is dead and science [is] always going marching along. Chevruel was not so much interested in those faint plum colored tones on the carrots or the carroty rust on the plums. He would have preferred those clearer tones that sometimes leap at you out of Demuth drawings like the healing rays recommended by our more expensive physicians.

I should think, indeed, these watercolors might have curative properties. You hear of stranger things. I can testify myself to having a slight relapse in health after being accidentally separated from one of my Demuths. Slight twinges of rheumatism developed, and that's a fact. One of my drawings, lent to a friend, got locked up in storage with all his things when he went to Europe, and it will be a year before he returns with the key and I can attempt to

[1]Nineteenth-century French color theorist Marcel Eugene Chevruel, who influenced Georges Seraut and other Pointillist painters.

prove my theory and cure my pains with an application of pure color.

But can Demuth be modern, you ask, if Marin is? Why not? The oddest fallacy amid all those that persist is that there must be a formula for modern art. Both men connect with the times, though they connect differently. The submerged, inner life of Marin revolts at science and fights it. But the science that kills Marin keeps Demuth alive. Demuth chants the Hymn Intellectual, as Walt Whitman would say.

In addition to the watercolors that have made Demuth one of the half dozen best known artists in the land there are some oils. One of them is a vigorously drawn Calla sprouting from a handsome sea shell. Just what it is that makes the Calla so esteemed in these days, other than the fact that it was considered vulgar a generation ago, I cannot say, but possibly that in itself is sufficient reason. The present seems determined to call the lie to everything in the past.

I have heard, though the rumor has not been affirmed, that this Bronzino-like portrait of a particularly robust Calla was intended by the artist as a tribute to the memory of a strange, erratic figure in the theatrical world who recently passed, as they say, to his reward.[1] This is as it should be. I believe in "homages" and sometimes wonder that the artists, who are supposed to be so desperately searching for subjects, do not indulge in them oftener. Here, where the streets are not very often named after painters and sculptors, other pictures, at least, may be. Mr. Demuth, to do him justice, has painted several such tributes to contemporary artists—among them John Marin, Arthur Dove and Georgia O'Keeffe—and includes them in his present show.

[1]American transvestite entertainer Bert Savoy; Demuth's letters do not make this identification, nor was it ever exhibited as a poster portrait of Savoy.

CHARLES DEMUTH

by A. E. Gallatin (New York: William Edwin Rudge, 1927)

[. . .] In my book on the American Water-Colourists, published in 1922, mention was made of the fact that Charles Demuth was not represented in any of the public museums. Happily, that state of affairs no longer prevails: since then Demuth's water-colours have been added to the permanent collections of the Metropolitan Museum of Art, the Art Institute of Chicago, the Fogg Museum of Harvard University, the Brooklyn Museum, the Cleveland Museum and the Rochester Museum. His water-colours have also been acquired by the semi-public Barnes Foundation, at Merion, Pennsylvania, and Phillips Memorial Gallery, at Washington.

The Barnes Foundation owns over fifty examples, including many of the vaudeville subjects, as well as a number of the illustrations. These were purchased shortly after the time of their execution. Mr. Ferdinand Howald's comprehensive collection of the vital contemporary American painters, probably the most important that has been formed, includes over thirty Demuths, choice and varied examples of the artist's work. Eventually this collection, together with a number of contemporary French pictures, is to be offered to the Columbus Museum. [. . .]

This steady acquisition of Demuths by the museums is certainly a very encouraging sign, for even that rare being, the curator with a flair for art, in addition to his antiquarian knowledge, finds that politics and the dead hand of officialdom are both exceedingly difficult things to set aside. What would happen to the artist in the socialist state it is not very agreeable to contemplate. If the state and the museums continued to give their patronage exclusively to the types of painters and sculptors whom they now encourage, the true artist no doubt would very shortly disappear. It is invariably the private collector who purchases the paintings by the genuine artists. [. . .]

On the other hand, when museums buy contemporary art in an intelligent manner, as some of them are now buying Demuths and as they will some day buy Marins, of course they are pursuing the right course. In that event a museum enjoys not only the distinction of having been adventurous and of buying at a time when it as possible to buy really fine examples, when the choice was greater and the prices more advantageous, but above all of having done something for the artist and the whole cause of modern art. [. . .]

It is interesting to note the great attraction which water-colour has had for the contemporary American painter, several of the most important of whom have chosen this medium almost to the exclusion of oil, while still others have executed a considerable part of their work in water-colour. Indeed, this preference for water-colour is nothing new in the history of American painting, as such names as those of Winslow Homer, much of whose most important work was executed in water-colour. Whistler and Sargent bear witness.

Aside from his etchings, which are important, made for the most part some years ago, and perhaps half a dozen essays in pastel or oil, John Marin's exhibited work has been executed exclusively in water-colour. Charles Demuth, one of the most highly gifted of living water-colourists, and the subject of this essay, has painted in both oil and in tempera, but water-colour has been his chief concern, and his fame no doubt will largely rest upon his work in this medium. The talented Charles Burchfield, the inimitable portrayer of sordid railway junction towns and amazing main streets of mid-western towns, very rarely works in any medium but water-colours. Preston Dickinson, who has brilliantly interpreted such subjects as the new architectural forms created by groups of factories, and the lately deceased Maurice Prendergast, a painter of authority, with a fine sense of decoration, are artists whose allegiance has been perhaps about equally divided as regards the employment of oil and water-colour. This is also true of Jules Pascin, American at least by naturalization; his finely organized drawings, in pencil or in ink, washed with water-colour, are perhaps of even more importance than his delicate paintings in oil.

Marin and Demuth, the most important figures in contemporary American painting, have evolved their forms in altogether different manners. Their temperaments differ as much as do the results of their investigations. Marin's water-colours are at times as lyrical as the poetry of Shelley, at other times they are dynamic in pent-up energy. They have been washed-in rapidly in the white heat of inspiration. Demuth's drawings are always most carefully and beautifully organized. He has aimed at perfection, which usually he has obtained. His water-colours and paintings are as fine in form and as delicately wrought as the essays of Max Beerbohm.

Charles Demuth was born at Lancaster, Pennsylvania, in 1883. He studied for some time at the Pennsylvania Academy of the Fine Arts in Philadelphia, after which, in 1912, he left for Paris, where he continued his studies for a period of a little less than two years. It was soon after this that the artist's talent began to develop into a personal expression and the remarkable series of illustrations for various works of fiction and drawings of vaudeville performers were started, shortly after his return to America. He continued to work on these drawings from time to time for the next five years, but has not produced any further work in this vein since 1919.

The period of the illustrations and vaudeville drawings, while the first in the artist's development, proved to be one of the most important, for some of Demuth's very finest things are to be found in these two sets of water-colours,. The imaginative drawings which illustrate various works of fiction, by French, American and German authors, have not been published with their accompanying text. Their interest, it is not quite necessary to note, is of course an aesthetic one and it is not because they are illustrations that we derive pleasure from them, any more than we do from Aubrey Beardsley's. Demuth's and Beardsley's illustrations interest us as independent works of art. [. . .]

In executing these illustrations the artist has first made a drawing outlined in pencil, upon which he has imposed washes of colour. His line is extremely sensitive and nervous, and the washes of delicate and alluring colour play an important part in organizing the design. The essence of the scene has in each case been portrayed. This is also true of the series of drawings of acrobats, dancers and other vaudeville performers, of which there are some eighty or ninety. Drawn at Lancaster, where the artist lives, these water-colours have been executed in much the same spirit as the illustrations. The use of contrasting backgrounds has in these drawings been employed to great advantage. They are enlivened with flashes of wit and especially in the vaudeville series there is that sense of reality and throb of life which one is always conscious of in the marvellous drawings made at the theatre and dance-hall by Toulouse-Lautrec.

Demuth's studies of flowers are no doubt the examples of his work which are most familiar to the public, for since the earliest days of his career he has been engrossed in the delineation of flower forms, and this interest shows no signs of abating. These water-colours the artist has produced in great profusion. The earlier ones are sometimes almost dainty in appearance, but as the years have passed they have taken on new and richer forms. His renderings of clusters of tulips, zinnias, cyclamen, daisies, gladioli and native pink orchids are possessed of a strange beauty, and that undefinable thing known as quality abounds in them. At times the wash is positively waxy in its subtle modulations, at other times the colour glows. Very often the curved forms of contrasting colour which compose the background and knit the design together show us what a genuine contribution to art was made by the Cubists and of what service their theories have been to the majority of the worthwhile men painting to-day. An intelligent use of the investigations of the Cubists is also discernible in the artist's interpretation of factories and other buildings, but, as in the studies of flowers, this influence is seen more especially in the backgrounds. The drawings of houses which the artist made in Bermuda are beautifully felt and set down with exquisite taste, notably successful in design and possessing passages of delicate and entrancing colour. Studying them, one thinks of the dictum of Sir Francis Bacon: "There is no exquisite beauty without some strangeness in the proportion." Becoming absorbed, as have a number of other American painters, with the distinctly new and original notes to be found in contemporary American architecture, but in his case especially as expressed in the construction of factories and mills, Demuth evidently came to the conclusion that oil and tempera were more appropriate media for the delineation of lofty chimneys, iron girders, and red brick façades than the more fragile medium of water-colour. These unlovely things, belonging so distinctly to our era of commercialism and mass production, have been made lovely by Demuth's rare art. Including several other pictures, among them paintings of colonial churches, there are about forty of these paintings, about half of them executed in oil and about half in tempera. They are, if anything, even more conspicuous for their precision of execution than the water-colours. Not only beautiful on account of their harmony and unity, these paintings of modern industrial America would at times almost seem to strike a note of gaiety. The titles, too, are witty, as witness such a one as that given to the painting of the two great chimneys which side by side rear themselves against a pale blue sky: *Aucassin and Nicolette.* One recalls, with great satisfaction, the uproar and indignation this title caused in academic circles. These pictures, it may be noted, were painted for the most part at Coatesville, an industrial town in Pennsylvania,[1] and at

[1]See page 153, footnote 1.

Provincetown. Another of the paintings is the only picture Demuth made during his visit to Paris in 1921, an interesting view of a street, patterned with windows, which bears the title *Rue du Singe qui Pèche*. This picture is in tempera: another, in oil, painted immediately after the artist's return to America, is the *Paquebot Paris,* two of her three red funnels outlined against the sky.

Quite recently Demuth has been turning his attention to the painting of still-life subjects, with fruits and vegetables as the motives. These water-colours mark a new phase in his development. The compositions, for one thing, have become rather more ambitious, his sheets of paper decidedly larger. The artist's technique has undergone certain changes as well. These still-lifes are very handsome and take their place with the artist's finest things. It is possible, however, that certain of Demuth's admirers find more charm in the flower subjects, with their note of graciousness. These fruits and vegetables are very cool. The juiciness of a peach by Renoir or the passion which Cézanne put into an apple are not to be found here. This is not voluptuous fruit: it comes from a country whose *vin du pays* is iced water.

No note on Demuth's work would be complete without reference to a set of four paintings which the artist executed in 1924—*hommages* to John Marin and three other painters.[1] These are very lively and entertaining canvasses, fine examples of craftsmanship and splendid in colour. I agree with Henry McBride that in this country there should be more homage done to artists by artists than there is. In France, they order these matters far better, as Mr. Yorick of [Laurence] Sterne's *Sentimental Journey* once said on another occasion. Not only the artist-painters, but the politicians as well. Indeed, were New York Paris, no doubt but that a portion of Broadway eventually would become, at least for a time, Boule-

[1]Georgia O'Keeffe, Arthur Dove, and Charles Duncan.

vard John Marin, a segment of Park Avenue Charles Demuth. Which would be rather nice.

WATER-COLOURS BY CHARLES DEMUTH

by Henry McBride, Creative Art, September 1929

Ask almost anyone conversant with art conditions in America: "Who are our six outstanding artists?" and the answer is more than likely to include the name of Demuth—Charles Demuth. This opinion, on investigation, is found to rest upon his achievement in water-colours, and especially upon a series devoted to still-life and flower-pieces. There are some paintings in oil and some water-colours on architectural and figure themes (prized possessions of some special Demuth enthusiasts, though not generally known), but the reputation has been fixed by the cool, clear, sure, elegant studies of fruits, vegetables and flowers. That they are "modern" does not seem to disturb many who are usually afflicted by what is known as "modernity"; that they are clear and understandable does not offend the progressives. In other words, Demuth enjoys a genuine success with his contemporaries, a quiet, steady unsensational success. I have never heard of any riots produced by his exhibitions nor voices raised in criticism of them.

In my little list of qualifying adjectives I employed purposely last the word "elegant," wishing it to have the emphasis of a last word. I don't believe Demuth himself would disavow that his mind, from a strictly modern base, reaches out continually for eighteenth century refinements. In fact, I have heard him confess that Fragonard was, and had been, the maddest passion of his *vie intellectuelle.*

Demuth's modernity is not something he has carved roughly from experience, but rather it is an accepted language of the day that he found waiting for him on the scene when he arrived. He adopted it easily and unconcernedly and without the sense of shame that attended the efforts of certain older men, such as Arthur B. Davies, Charles Rosen, etc., who changed in mid-career from the old style to the new. It is because of his own perfectly natural participation in contemporary thought about nature that his flashing, geometrically arranged skies beating down upon disintegrated and recomposed Christopher Wren steeples escape the contumely that is heaped upon most modern art in America.

When the flower pictures had already made Demuth known and it had become fashionable to own one, Mr. Daniel, who was then Mr. Demuth's merchant, showed us all, surreptitiously, some figure drawings. They were not precisely shocking, but one or two of the drawings illustrated points in Zola's *Nana,* and just before the war we were still sufficiently Victorian to shudder at the thought of exposing pictures of reprehensible *Nana* on the walls of a public gallery. Times, of course, have greatly changed since then and now *Nana,* poor dear, can go anywhere she wants to, but by the time our collectors had realized that "Nanas" had become perfectly all right, and rather better company than most, the entire lot of Mr. Demuth's figure drawings had been swept into some especially well-hidden collection—and it was announced that the artist was not to do any more figures! This was a real blow. Most amateurs, now that *Nana* had definitely come and gone, had decided that in Demuth we had some one who could do for us what Toulouse-Lautrec had done for the French. But it was not to be. Demuth, they told us, was ill; so ill that his alarmed friends actually thought a "finis" had been written to the career. I put the question to Demuth after he was restored to apparent health, "why he didn't try some figure things?" and in a short reply, looking in another direction, he answered, "I no longer seem to have the energy."

And in the meantime the still-lifes and flower-pieces continue. The fuzzy bloom on the peach, the glittering polish of the aubergine, the controlled richness of the opulent zinnias, all these and other such splendours from the vegetable world inform the new Demuth water-colours with a style that it rejoices one to see appreciated. They appear to be the best things in that line that we have done.

DEMUTH WATERCOLORS AND OILS AT "AN AMERICAN PLACE"

by Angela E. Hagen, Creative Art, June 1931

Among the figure drawings in aquarelle seen in this exhibition, mainly illustrations to a novel of Henry James, hung a representation of an eighteenth century French interior, illustrating one of the *Imaginary Portraits* of Walter Pater. Mr. Demuth mentioned that he at one time intended illustrating all of the Portraits of this delightful book. His interest in Walter Pater seems significant. Like the writer of the former generation who still lives for us through his *Renaissance* and *Marius,* Mr. Demuth has a highly sensitive, intuitive way of feeling himself into the life of things and persons. His delicate medley of field flowers is unique in its combination of structure, precision, and yet a sense of delicious and careless bloom. Only a mind of great refinement could understand and interpret the nature of each species of plant as it is here done—each flower speaks in its own language, as it were, bluebells in finest precision of form, miniature daisies in their native full roundness, another theme, of daffodils, reproduces this plant's lush and yet airy golden fullness, and again lilies wind themselves out of their soil to develop their great concave bloom. Underneath this beauty of growing life is a realization of structure learnt probably from Cézanne and from the artist's own intuition. This sense saves the flower paintings, as everything else the artist accomplishes, from any "sweetness" or insipidity. Fruit and vegetable, too, are rendered in clear color and deeply understood form; still-life, which is anything but "still" and, as to many an artist, has revealed also to this man the life behind the quiet surface, retreated, perhaps (except to the eye of the initiated), but never "still"!

The illustrations to Henry James (never used as such) are, of course, perfectly independent creations, using situations from the novel as a point of departure to upbuild the world of Charles Demuth. And, on a fine, small scale what an astonishing world is revealed in these amazingly accomplished watercolors! The drama of the situations lies not in the attitudes or gestures of these people, but in the complexities of thought and emotion that seem in the calligraphy of the fine drawing with which the washes are combined, actually to live and weave through space, from person to person. Rare and subtle in color, meaning, composition. They were painted twelve or fourteen years ago. One longs for a renaissance of this type of the artist's work.

The oil paintings are of recent date. Casual observation reveals a new, a different world. Only deeper study traces these canvases to fundamentals of character and vision that mark the earlier watercolors. We might call them highly sublimated posters, or we might call them phantasies of precision (if that were not too paradox) or "études" in paint, as we have the musical masters' logical, severe studies. They defy their own commonplace subjects (houses bearing signs of feed and grain dealers, ships' funnels, a stark water tower, a maze of telegraph wires stretched between shacks, etc.) by their immaculate workmanship (a jeweler could not finish surfaces more finely), transforming these commonplaces, not as Corot in early years transformed a red brick factory building into a vibrating loveliness of color and light, but into highly ordered logical arrangements. The commonplace, in fact, is pursued to some last conclusion, that reveals its mystical contents. Isolated figures and letters grow, even when rendered with hard sign-painters' gold, into significance and meaning, that certain cults have invested in numbers. The wires that stretch through space as taut lines are somehow related to Paul Klee's drawings. Again the fine surface and drastically simplified forms are reminiscent of Georgia O'Keeffe. Although this work is interesting and free from formula, we would like to think of it as a phase in this gifted artist's development, leading to a broader, fuller, more vital expression, of which this fine man is so capable.

PEN PORTRAITS: CHARLES DEMUTH: ARTIST

by Rita Wellman, Creative Art, December 1931

We were students together when we were very young. When we were very young, we were very old. We were all bored with life; knew everything there was to know, and only condescended to give our time and talents to painting because it seemed to our jaded spirits the one respectable calling left.

Demuth was out of my class entirely. Already he had started on his own bent, while my own dream of Heaven, fame, glory and beautiful experience was to achieve an X on a charcoal drawing which would mean that it met with the approval of that splendid man and teacher, Thomas Anshutz. (I forgot to say that all this took place at the Pennsylvania Academy of the Fine Arts, Philadelphia). Clearly out of my class. Whatever Demuth's theories were, what his aims, who were his heroes and who his Black Beasts I did not know. Since he tells me today that he has none of these things, perhaps he had not then. As I remember them and their work I doubt if he was much influenced by any of the artists whose profession it was to inspire, guide, or gently dissuade from their purpose the collection of individuals who had gathered under the ramblings roofs of the Academy of Art's name.

A little man was the giant among the instructors, William

M[erritt] Chase. He looked like a little French banker with his gray goatee, pince-nez, white piqué vest and white spats; a ring with a ruby in it around the knot of his four-in-hand tie, usually red. We had a model in the life-class who looked like a Piero della Francesca madonna with the figure of a Rubens' Venus. Someone painted a corner of the life-class with the students in shadow and Chase and Lena, her name was Lena, in bright light; Chase with his hat on, in his dapper little business suit, a carnation in his buttonhole, pointing his stick at Lena, leaning her weight on that monstrous, patient model's right hip. I wonder if Demuth painted this picture. Lena's hip and the carnation might have been done by him.

[Hugh] Breckenridge, the man whose paintings always looked like lighted matches no matter what the subject was, was an excellent still-life man. If Demuth got anything from him it must have been a very useful lesson not to have anything to do with lighted matches. Henry McCarter was a man of fascination and imagination and a provocative teacher. I remember one day when criticizing one of my drawings he looked up at me, quite kindly, and asked, "Do you ever try to write stories?" Charles Demuth must have received a great deal of stimulus from this artist, certainly a great deal of encouragement and appreciation. The latter, in a nest of hornets, a den of wild beasts, a cave full of destroyers such as any art school is, must have helped. Or perhaps things worked just the other way around. Sometimes it is the hornets and beasts and destroyers who help, the most. If you survive their onslaughts, both silly, pretentious and violently antagonistic, you at least know where you are, with only the next thing to find out, *who* you are. This, Demuth seems to have done surprisingly early. It would be difficult to detect the influences of other artists or schools in his work. Recently, the canvases like *My Egypt* show a more pronounced modernism than earlier things of this painter of flowers and clowns, but even in these newer paintings the expression is purely individualist.

[Alfred] Stieglitz, who took an interest in Demuth when he first came back from Paris with more paintings in his head than in his luggage—Paris would have this effect upon him—got up his first comprehensive one-man show this year. But it was Charles Daniel, perhaps even more courageous with untried painters than Stieglitz, who was the first to exhibit Demuth's watercolor drawings and canvases shortly after his return from Paris.

The reason, probably, why he didn't paint in Paris is because he paints at home. His house is in Lancaster, not far—but far enough—from Philadelphia. The Demuths have lived here since Charles Demuth was a child. He has known it so long he doesn't have to be bothered with any feeling about it. When he wants to work, there it is, as it always was, the place which shuts out the world and leaves him alone with the job on hand. The house stands in that part of the country where those strange religious sects flourish. I never know whether they are Quakers, Mennonites, Shakers or all three, or whether or not they are all pacifists, who have a silent service at church and who sew engaged pairs together in a blanket in order to find out if this kind of proximity agrees with them. The Demuths have never belonged, as far as the artist knows, to this sect or any of its branches. The house is of red brick, handmade, and there are handsome black trimmings on the façade. Charles Demuth talks of selling the bricks some day, as one talks of selling the family jewels—more in pride of possession than out of any actual intention.

The interior is filled with Victorian heirlooms arranged with perverse quaintness by Robert Locher and Demuth. The studio is the same room which was fled to one day when the small Charles decided he wanted to be alone in order to put down on a sheet of drawing paper what he wanted to remember about a flower he had picked in his mother's garden. (His mother has that magic with flowers which belongs to a few rare individuals.) His mother's sewing machine was in it then, and is still there.

Edward Hopper should paint it some day—this storeroom of discarded things, the white-washed walls, the camp bed, the Lautrec lithograph—and he should put Charles Demuth sitting in a corner huddled over a drawing, catch him as he looks up with that expression of his, as of a kind of hurt ferocity.

Charles Demuth paints in Lancaster. He does nothing else where. When he feels he wants to see people he comes to New York. After three or four days of seeing people he decides it is time to go back to Lancaster, Pennsylvania. He is not home-loving, nor anti-social. Lancaster fits, and when something fits it is a good idea to keep to it, if you have work to do. Demuth has no particularly violent dislikes, unless it be arguments. The other day we both agreed that this was our favorite hate, although we had different reasons for hating arguments and shying from arguers. We had quite an argument about it. He likes horses, movies (when they contain Charlie Chaplin and Marlene Dietrich), wine, Marcel Duchamp, swans, Diego di Rivera, Marcel Proust, prize-fights, Robert Locher. He does not care for domestic pets nor for small children, nor people who talk about art. He prefers the wooden and plush era to the modern metal and leather one, and cannot be enthusiastic about the creations of any modern decorators, with the exception of Djo Bourgeois. Locher is his friend, but he admires his modern work less than his earlier work. He does not understand women nor classic music. He knows flowers.

He thinks it would be wonderful for him to illustrate an edition of Marcel Proust. So do I. We spoke of certain scenes. "Think of Odette in that funny, stuffy apartment near the beginning. The wicker furniture. Odette in a long negligee, pink chiffon with ostrich plumes down the front—the catelyas!" "The

Duchess de Geurmantes in that hat trimmed with violets." "Odette in the Bois, wearing more catelyas." He should do it.

from FAREWELL, CHARLES

by Marsden Hartley, The New Caravan, 1936

No one wants to see death stalking in the wake of his friends as persistently as I have been obliged to do of late.

I don't recover from these episodes as quickly as some are inclined to do, accepting them as plain facts of life, and I am still wanted to vibrant companionship of those who have brought either richness or fun, or both, into my being. Charles is only just gone, and our private airs still resound with wave-length sharpness of his so recent presence.

Charles has only just gone, rest his winsome bones; I will proceed to the period of twenty-three years ago, the place is Paris, the time is nineteen twelve-thirteen, and the hour of first meeting a certain déjeuner at the Restaurant Thomas, on the Boulevard Montparnasse. [. . .]

At [. . .] a certain déjeuner, the restaurant was crowded, and for the purpose of regaling Charles's memory as if he were here, and how do we know he isn't, for I am sure all my friends are around a corner somewhere, and so my sense of mourning for physical losses never lasts very long, which is of course very nice and pleasant. . . .

I shall recall [. . .] to him the day he ambled up to our table, and because of a hip infirmity he had invented a special sort of ambling walk which was so expressive of him, there being one place left at the table at which we all sat, asking if he might sit with us, the request being granted without further thought.

It wasn't long before Charles made us particularly aware of him by a quaint, incisive sort of wit with an ultra sophisticated, post-eighteen-ninety touch to it, for I always felt that Charles's special personal tone had been formed with this period, the murmur of imagined deaths of superior trifles clinging to his very sensitive hands, and a wistful comprehension of what many a too tender soul has called infectious sin, alas how harmless [. . .].

Charles, dressed always in the right degree of good taste, English taste of course, carrying his cane elegantly and for service, not for show, as he had always the need of a cane, coming to our table as I have said, we all saying yes of course, and there was immediately much quaint banter afloat, interspersed with veiled sous endentus, all of it fun, and I remember saying to Charles after the meal was over, I think you had better come and sit with us all the time, and so it was Charles became known to me over the space of the ensuing twenty-three years, giving now the touch of immortality to the many little bits of fun and droll waggery.

Charles was, as we all now know, a fine painter, he had a true painter's cultivation, he had a real feeling for esthetic values even if he thought of them a little preciously perhaps, he was nevertheless a true artist, and with all that a gay playmate.

Charles, like so many of us, became part of a certain epoch in phase of art history in America, beginning with that remarkable and never repeated summer at Provincetown where the Provincetown Players began their first memorable attempt at little theatre movement. [. . .]

Charles in the midst of all this, especially in the evening or the long night sessions when after the various kinds of "office hours" peculiar to us all were over playtime was likewise a matter of big business, and as I see it now, an excellent good time was had by all—all of it provocative of hilarity and tiger-like stalking after amusement. [. . .]

Charles liked being in on these parties, those tiger-like stalkings after amusement down the courses of the night, he liked being swept into atmospheres and getting his own funny kick out of them and they were big ideas and issues for Charles, bringing some of the best of his work out of him, and I am sure he gave them farreaching importance by virtue of the fact that his imagination was essentially of the spiral variety.

Charles was doing somewhere about this time the series of witty water colours of acrobats, sailors in wild pursuit, ladies in quest of submarine favours, motives which I always felt ended too soon, as they brought so much of the fun out of him, and from these he veered over to Henry James's *Turn of the Screw,* which fine drawings did as much probably as any of his efforts to establish him in his place in the prevailing art history of America.

It was in that other famous nineteen-twenty period in Paris [. . .] that another phase of bohemian history was created.

Charles loved Paris, the Paris which had always given him so much unalloyed satisfaction, and it certainly had quality then, which we now hear is irrevocably lost.

Charles seemed always, in a way, to suffer his thrills, he seemed sort of lashed with ecstasies then pacified, he seemed to sort of tremble at the approach of them, succumb to the magic of their reality, and like so many intensive natures regret their departure into the realms of memory, setting about to recapture in the imagination their appreciable beauty, to be made good use of in some form or other.

The picture turns now to a moment in an upper room of the Hotel Lutetia on Raspail, finding Charles looking out of a given and what has always seemed to me that remarkable dormer window which afforded one of the most amazing views of Paris to be had anywhere on the Left Bank, and this room and window therefore, always sought by him.

It was a visual operatic Paris that one beheld, and I can never fathom just how this angle was obtained, but you had to a striking degree, all that Paris had to offer, or most all. [. . .]

Charles is at the right of this amazing dormer window, I at the left, and the disheartening news has been revealed, he saying to me, and I recall it so well—O well, I've seen it all—I've done it all, and the throat thickened with the sense of a sudden revealment—Charles learns that he is really ill, and that he must go home.

Summer was on the way to being over, he booked passage home to begin the scientific experiments with the now so famous insulin treatment, being one of the first patients, and as he was the inheritor of its virtues, for it let him live fifteen years longer than he assumed he could, he was also inheritor of its dangerous variations, for he never knew when he would be overtaken with those violent and terrifying collapses, due chiefly to neglect in punctuality of regime.

Charles had a flair for the frivolities, but they had to be of elegant tone, a little precious in their import, swift in their results, he spent hours chasing phantoms of an aristocratic nature, and was over overcome by the highly defined appearance of things, they must come, let's say, adhering to the note in their quality as Truffles de Perigord, or—costly to his imagination, he thought of things as interesting only by the degree of excitement they held for them, to get his own kick out of them. He was a bit proustian in this, he liked fragile gossip, he liked the flair of à la mode emotions, he liked superficialities, but with the difference that being a serious person, he understood the vast implications of the little secrets of life, he rubbed his hands so to speak, if he came close enough to the thin surfaces of them—he was not strictly speaking, flaneur, but he liked the picture of life which such a position offered.

Charles's home life in Lancaster, Pa., will give you the solid background of his rich simplicity.

His mother must be brought into the picture with tender regard, for she is one of those fine old householders in a small Pennsylvania town, so fastidious about the order of her home that she does everything herself as part of the noble rites of existence.

She went, formerly to least, with the manner of a lady who can trust no servant for qualities, to buy her own provender, she would be at the Mennonite market among the earliest, never later than six in the morning, because she wanted the dew on those fresh greens, she bought this or that of her special Mennonite, for these are the people of this region, those sternly simple people dressed in the long black garb of the cult,[1] as if each were the special bishop of his parish, and the greens were so precious looking they seemed more like corsages than edibles, and a basket of them would have set a chef of the Cordon Bleu to gloating with culinary glee over them.

In the midst of this rich domestic milieu Charles was reared, and when he was at home he liked it thoroughly, as when he was abroad he liked the usual variations of such character.

He spent, because he had a talent for decoration, much of his time making the quaint and typical brick house on King Street, behind which the so typical church stands that forms one of the best of his subjects in his larger paintings,[2] into all but a de luxe affair inside, and though I did not see it after the renovation, report records its charm and the exactitude of detail, for the kind of the house that it is. It belongs to the era of shell flowers, wax fruit, painted velvet, bead-encrusted antimacassars, and the usual complement of horsehair, bell pulls, opaque glass, silver lustre, and all the lavish profusion of accessory of such periods. [. . .]

We of the intimate crew are all familiar with the patrician hands of Charles, they were Chinese in character, the fingers long and slender, belonging to that species of hands that though they live the life of every other sort of hands living a life occupied with common things seem to be living a life of their own, and I am

[1]Both Mennonite and Amish cultures supply Lancaster's weekly market with fresh produce.

[2]Trinity Lutheran Church, visible from the windows of Demuth's house.

thinking here of hands such as those of Georgia O'Keeffe, Robert Locher, Zasu Pitts,[2] the family of amazing hands as it were, the incredibly wistful hands of Zasu Pitts which we all know, before they become subjected to trade values.

Charles's hands were unusual, and some of us will miss them, how the Chinese would have fêted them, even Charles's whole appearance was at times permeated with oriental stillness. Until it woke to express a world unlike all that, and became for the moment, average.

Charles had respect for the sentimental, he believed he had been true to the Cynara of his perceptions, he liked nacreous whisperings such as are to be found in the delicate work of that other hypersensitive Charles, in the English esthetic world, Charles Conder, whose deepest wonder brought forth nothing heavier than a fan, or fine touches on silk.

It takes time to tell all of what one knows of an intimate, and I have been happily that, in this case for a period of twenty-three years—and the purpose here has been only to outline some of the outstanding traits and tricks of one who liked to be admired, and certainly, himself, enjoyed and admired avidly; he had a capacity for admiration as well as friendship, he believed in friends and was amply supplied with them, a nice old-fashioned quality that survives, regardless of the whims and trends of life.

As for his works of art, they attest to themselves, they are always in the best of taste, conscious of good tradition, a perhaps too concrete insistence upon the elements of refinement and grace, delicate to the last, chiefly flower pieces, because they were within range of his later failing energies, he never could abide the vulgarities in the world of flower painting produced by a powerful painter like Courbet, who has no trace of feeling for them at all.

Charles never made a bad picture, and he made a lot of very

[1]Film actress best remembered as Trina in Erich von Stroheim's *Greed,* 1926.

good ones, and if many of his pictures were frail in substance they were true in import, essentially decorative, fastidious in line, harmonious, possibly to excess.

He was no cheap arriviste, he was no intense eclectic, so there is no strain in his product.

The transition from the earlier, superiorly illustrative subjects to the later, cubistically evolved realistic pictures, is all one thing, and there is, therefore, a natural sequence in his product.

Charles loved the language of paint with the fervour of an ardent linguist, and this side of his work alone, is thoroughly achieved.

We see of late that he has inherited, like O'Keeffe, a following of copyists, but that will disturb no one, for the difference is acutely evident.

I would say, that all in all, Charles had a good time being himself, he probably sweated copious romantic tears to get at the vital incisive values of his experience like so many other idealists, but he did not have to descend to the miseries for the revelation of his powers.

Something like a master of the comic insinuation which lies within and behind so much average experience, always the living material of the fool or the saint at our disposal. Charles traversed the all in all thin area of esthetic experience with a firm step, and he left footprints here and there which have long since been measured and found of the proper size.

DEMUTH MEMORIAL EXHIBITION

by Henry McBride, New York Sun, 18 December 1937

The memorial exhibition in the Whitney Museum of the late Charles Demuth is astonishingly reassuring. All the drawings look valuable and desirable. This is largely because they are well shown. The Demuth water colors are unlike other American water colors and the Whitney Museum is unlike other American museums. The two go well together.

Demuth's art is precious or it is nothing. If you will see actual jewels in a museum you will know what I mean. Emeralds and diamonds that glow with conscious value upon a lady's finger suddenly become cold and lifeless when transposed to a vitrine in a museum.

Possession and intimacy are necessary to a Demuth water color.

The Whitney Museum is a reconstruction from several dwellings that must have been exceedingly comfortable in their time, and certain of the galleries retain a warm and agreeable "residence" feeling.[1] One of them, on the second floor, is a symphony in tones of rose, luxuriously carpeted and with perfect window curtains, and in this room the loveliest of the flower paintings are shown. Or is it that they are the best? Might it not be that the flower pictures relish their pleasant surroundings and perform well because of them? I am inclined to think that is it. The entire exhibition is seductive and, due to the clearness and distinction of the workmanship, is bound to be a popular success, but one or two of the rooms have the white walls that are necessary for strictly modern pictures, and on them some of the Demuth drawings have that jewels-in-a-museum look that has been referred to. Burglars who rob museums are, of course, very reprehensible persons, yet any method that brings a museum jewel back into private circulation is not altogether to be despised.

The anticipated public favor that is to be allotted to this exhibition is a curious instance of what an artist can do with his public once he has gained a public, for Demuth practiced many devices that are not forgiven to all American painters. For instance, many persons who condemn cubism as the sin of all sins, have openly admired the several water color versions of Sir Christopher Wren church steeples without seeming to be aware

[1]In 1927, the Whitney Museum was still located in what had been opulent private residences at 8 West Eighth Street in Greenwich Village.

that the drawings are cubistic. It is quite refined and delicate cubism but it is cubism just the same. Then there are the series of illustrations to novels by Henry James and Zola which have acquired a great deal of local fame, and which some critics (myself included) rate as the best things that Demuth did, and yet they are calligraphic; and officialdom in America doesn't yet know what calligraphic draftsmanship is and consequently is bound to disapprove of it for at least ten years to come. On top of these there is a whole roomful of stylized symbols, headed by the *I Saw The Figure 5 in Gold,* which looks so handsome, as now shown, that I'll wager any sum you mention that the average man from the street will forget to be mystified by it. And yet, as a rule, we New Yorkers do not care for mystical pictures. This special permission to the artist to do as he pleased was won by the delightful flower studies, which radiated such an air of "sweetness and light," especially when owned, that their admirers quickly began to feel that Demuth could do no wrong.

At the same time this cubism, this calligraphy, and this symbolism are not especially creative and that is probably the reason why they are so little challenging. Cubism and calligraphy were simply part of the art-jargon in the period in which he grew up and he used them just as he used the current speech. Cubism was not necessary to him as it could have been, conceivably, to an artist who could accept the world on no other terms, but being very distinctly a citizen of the world he "played up" the fashions from Paris with a degree of amusement and certainly with great competence. He may be said to have translated cubism "into American," and to have added to it some of his native elegance.

Elegance was an insistent aspiration with him. He once told me that he admired Fragonard enormously and that the thought of Fragonard often guided his impulses. No reflections from Fragonard, however are visible in his work, unless you think the French master helped the distant American to some of his clarity. There is certainly enough elegance in the still life of *Grapes and Turnips,* shown in the entrance hall, to have guaranteed it an acceptance at the Court of Louis XIV in spite of the (perhaps) lowly turnips. In fact, these Demuth turnips are royal. No others in art match them.

The special concern of the students, however, is the opportunity provided by this event, to renew acquaintance with the Demuth illustrations to *The Turn of the Screw* and *The Beast in the Jungle,* by Henry James; illustrations that startled the art world a generation ago and then were promptly whisked away into private collections. These drawings are done in scribbled lines that would have horrified the pedantic followers of the Atelier Gérûme if they had not already been somewhat quelled and defeated by the cubistic revolutionaries of the day, but unprejudiced younger observers were so impressed by the Demuth intensity of feeling in these drawings that they did not recognize that method as calligraphic and succumbed to the horror, and morbidezza, and general screwiness that the artist had extracted from the fearsome novels. Since that day a whole school of young Americans have practiced calligraphy with an assiduity worthy of the Chinese, but these drawings by Demuth remain the most distinguished contributions yet made to this kind of expression.

INDEX

Page numbers in boldface indicate recipients of letters.